The
Parent Factor

The
Parent Factor

How our parents shape our self-concept, our perception of God, and our relationships with others...and how to re-shape false perceptions using the truth of God's Word.

Robert S. McGee
Jim Craddock
Pat Springle

Edited by Susan Joiner

Rapha Publishing
Houston, TX

We dedicate this book to those who read it, with our sincere desire that godly wisdom will be gained and lives will be blessed.

THE PARENT FACTOR

CONTENTS

CONTENTS

Acknowledgments

This book would not have been written without the support, encouragement, and hard work of several people. Many thanks to...

...Sandy Ballard, who meticulously and cheerfully typed the many revisions and revisions of revisions

...Dr. Ralph W. Neighbour, Jr., for his excellent work in getting this manuscript started

...Susan Joiner, who edited the manuscript to give it clarity and a smooth flow

...many of our friends who have struggled with their views of God and have seen genuine, life-changing progress

...and to our families, who have loved us, encouraged us, and modeled the character of God to us.

Introduction

A person's relationship with his parents is usually the most profound relationship of his life. It shapes his self-concept, his hopes, his dreams, his perceptions, his relationship with God, and his relationship with everyone else. It is hard to overestimate the depth and scope of the importance of his relationship with his parents. Sadly, many of us come from homes where we did not feel the affection or receive the encouragement and patient correction that a child needs. Our perception of God is colored and clouded by the neglect, abuse, and manipulation of our parents. We, in fact, assume that God is just like them; that He is neglectful, abusive, and manipulative, too. If our perception of God is wrong, then our primary source of wisdom, love, and strength is thwarted. We withdraw from Him. We don't trust Him. We are angry with Him. We feel alone and compelled to find fulfillment in other ways and through other relationships. But these alternatives only result in more pain and emptiness.

This book attempts to define and describe the way our perception of God has been shaped by our relationship with our parents. It shows how parental relationships affect our relationships with others and even with ourselves. But it doesn't stop there. It also identifies the truth of God's love and power, and suggests ways we can experience the reality of His character. It is through our true experience of Him that we can handle our other relationships correctly.

The workbook section of this book is particularly helpful. It is designed to help you reflect on the pains and joys in your life and also, to help you apply the truths of God's word in every emotion, dream, and relationship in your life.

These realizations are difficult to handle alone. We suggest that you find a friend or a small group of friends to go through the material with you. Their wisdom, encouragement, and affirmation will greatly benefit your ability to see substantive and long-lasting changes in your life. And you will be able to help them, too.

It is our hope that you will increasingly experience the reality of God, and that you will enjoy more intimacy, love, and acceptance than you have ever known!

SECTION I

THE PROBLEM: Perceptions of God are Shaped by Parents

One

THE SHAPING OF A CHILD

Children are supremely moldable. They each have their own God-given personalities, but their confidence and self-concept are shaped by their parents like lumps of clay in a potter's hands. If they feel loved, valued, protected, and are encouraged to try without the fear of condemnation when they fail, they are shaped into confident, secure people. If, however, children feel condemned by harsh, perfectionistic parents, or neglected by parents who are too preoccupied with their own selfish interests, the shaping of their childhood will produce adults who are plagued by insecurity, guilt, fear, anger, loneliness, and withdrawal, driven to please people and accomplish goals in the hope of winning their love.

Parents play the critical role in shaping a child's life. In his book, *The First Three Years of Life*, Harvard physician Dr. Burton White says that a child desperately needs the unbounded love, affection, and attention of his parents in order to develop emotional and relational health. Dr. White calls this "irrational love," and he states that no one can take the place of parents in communicating this kind of love and shaping and molding a child's life:

> *I have had the privilege of being able to compare the everyday experiences of very many children, from many kinds of families, and the evidence of my own observations is overwhelmingly that, all things being equal, a baby's parents are far more likely to meet his most important developmental needs than are any other people.* [1]

This book is not primarily focused on the goal of making you a better parent, though that is certainly one of its applications. This book is about you. It is designed to help you see how your life has been shaped by your parents. It focuses on how you have developed emotionally, relationally, and spiritually so that you can experience more of the freedom, grace, and strength of God in each of these areas of your life. To understand this critical process, let's look at the nature of children.

A young child (such as you when you were a child) gets his perception of reality by looking at his parents. By observing what they get excited or angry about, he learns what is important. By seeing how they relate to each other and to others, he learns about love and hate. By observing them, he learns about every significant issue in life. The child also ascribes god-like characteristics to his parents: what they say is Truth, what they demand is Law, and how they treat him is Love. If their words and actions are loving, protective, and compassionate, then the child is likely to experience good emotional, relational, and spiritual health. But if their words and actions are harmful and distorted, his perception of life will be painful and distorted, too. The accuracy of these perceptions and the warmth of the family environment shape the child in the critical areas of his self-concept, his relationships with others, and his view of God.

The Child's Self-Concept

If a child is consistently affirmed and disciplined in a loving way, he will probably grow up believing that he is a valuable and secure person. He will be able to take risks without the confining fear of failure, and he can enjoy relationships without the fear of intimacy.

If the child's need for love and acceptance is not met because his parents are condemning or neglectful, he may conclude that there is something wrong with him. (He probably will think that his parents are always right, so the fault must be his, not theirs.) Consequently, he will learn to condemn himself for not being worthy of being loved, and will either deny his need for love and acceptance, or try to win that love by his performance. If this self-condemnation is not stopped by consistent love, it can slowly evolve into a deeply rooted self-hatred.

Relating to Others

In a secure and loving environment, a child learns to give and receive love. He learns to experience the deep joys and pains of intimacy with other people.

In a relationship with condemning or manipulative parents, however, a child learns to condemn and manipulate others. He will whine until he gets his way. And, even as an adult, he may whine and complain until people either give in or withdraw from him. He may become a master manipulator, subtly and intricately using praise and condemnation to change others' behavior to suit himself. People then become objects used to meet his needs instead of individuals to be loved.

People tend to treat others in one of two ways: they either copy their parents' model of relationships or they attempt to be as unlike their parents as possible. One woman who had a harsh and abusive father became a very permissive mother. Most of us, however, tend to duplicate the behavior and relationships of our parents. Modeling is a powerful force in shaping the lives of children.

The Child's View of God

For better or for worse, parents represent God to their children. A child's emotional and spiritual foundations are to be provided by them. Most important of all, parents are to model the love and strength of God to their children. They are responsible for portraying His reliability, His unconditional love, His acceptance, and His purposeful discipline. A child's view of God is shaped by his or her parents.

Though it is obviously not possible for a parent to model the character of God perfectly, it is his responsibility to represent the Lord to his children. In the Scriptures, parents are instructed to have compassion for their children (Ps. 103:13), to train each child in the way most appropriate for that child (Prov. 22:6), to discipline firmly and with love

(Prov. 23:13-14), to avoid provoking them to anger (Eph. 6:4), and to teach and model the character, purposes, and instructions of God in everything said and done (Deut. 6:6-9). Clearly, it is God's design that parents reflect His love, protection, and provision to their children so that they will be secure and learn to love, trust, and serve the Lord wholeheartedly.

If the parents are preoccupied with their own selfish interests, if they are "too busy" for their children, or if they are abusive, condemning, or neglectful, the children will believe that God is just like them. He will be perceived as condemning instead of forgiving, cruel instead of loving, and neglectful instead of attentive.

Although parents play a major role in shaping the identity of their children, a positive home environment doesn't guarantee security and stability. One young woman with a strong and loving family had her confidence shattered by her peers in college. She became insecure and withdrawn. Conversely, poor parental modeling doesn't guarantee that children will be insecure. Two young brothers from an abusive family were taken in by a foster family. They experienced the healing of love and affirmation even though it wasn't from their parents. These are exceptions. But the pattern of parents shaping the identity of their children is still remarkably strong.

Children are indeed like lumps of clay that are molded by a potter's hands. Your life is a lump of clay that has been shaped and molded by your parents. It is our hope that God will profoundly use this book in your life to give you:

1. An *understanding* about why you feel and respond the way you do. Quite often, this understanding is a painful process, but objectivity is very important if progress is to be made.

2. A *process* of change to begin (or continue) to improve your view of God and your self-concept. The workbook section of this book is specifically designed to help you analyze your relationship with your parents, your view of God, and your

sense of self-worth, but it doesn't stop with self-analysis. Bible studies and thought questions are included to help you build a new and fresh belief system.

3.   A strong and vibrant *relationship* with God so that your life can be characterized by freedom, joyful obedience, and deep relationships with others.

[1]Burton L. White, *The First Three Years Of Life*, rev. ed. (Englewood Cliffs, NY: Prentice-Hall Press, 1985), p. 268.

Two

THE PARENT FACTOR

Your view of God, your self-concept, and your ability to relate to others are shaped by your relationship with your parents. If your parents were (and are) loving and supportive, then you probably believe that God is loving and strong. You're probably a secure and confident person, and are able to relate easily to other people. However, if your parents were harsh and demanding, you probably believe that God is also that way, and you may think that you can never do enough to please Him. Your insecurity may result in either a withdrawal from others or a defensiveness in relationships.

Whether they have been loving or aloof, kind or harsh, supportive or neglectful, your parents have played a major role in forming your view of God, your view of yourself, and your relationships with others. The results can be wonderful or tragic.

Supportive, Accepting Parents

I was once invited to a Bible study for young businessmen in Dallas. The group met at a restaurant in the morning before work. I don't want to say it was too early, but when we drove up, the other men were waiting in their cars because the restaurant hadn't opened yet! It was so early I wasn't even sure of what day it was. When the doors opened, I wondered if I could get the waitress to give me coffee intravenously in both arms and eyes. How many cups of coffee can eight guys drink at that hour?

About halfway through the Bible study, I became relatively coherent. We were looking at passages of Scripture which describe evangelism, and we talked about how to communicate the gospel in the marketplace.

These men really wanted to serve the Lord, and it was a lively discussion.

After an hour or so, several of the men had to go to work, and the group began to disband. One of them, Jim, who didn't have to go directly to his job, remained behind. He had been active in the discussion about evangelism; so, I asked him some questions about his relationship with the Lord. It must be strong, I surmised, if he had the confidence to share his faith regularly.

Jim described how he had become a Christian and how the Bible study was helping him to be effective in serving the Lord. I asked a question that I've learned to ask people like Jim: "The Lord said that those who are fruitful will be pruned so they can bear more fruit. How do you handle it when the Lord prunes you?"

He thought for a minute, and said, "I assume the Lord knows what is best for me, and He knows what I need to serve Him more effectively."

What a response! I turned to Frank, the Bible study leader, who could tell I was impressed–delighted–by Jim's answer. Frank said, "He really means it. He has an excellent perspective on the character of God."

I asked Jim, "How did you develop your view of God? It seems pretty clear and strong."

He responded, "Well, my parents have always been really loving toward me. I always knew I could count on them when I was growing up, and they disciplined me in a consistent and loving way. I guess I got my view of God by watching my parents."

As I learned more about Jim, I found that although he had to face issues with God as we all do, he had a peace about who he was. He knew there were changes to be made in his performance, but he accepted who he was. Finally, I saw the influence of his early parent-child relationship by his openness in relating to others.

Verbally Abusive Parents

I asked Cheryl to describe her home life. "It was okay," she said, not exactly giving the kind of full description I was looking for.

I probed a bit. "Tell me how your parents got along."

"Well, they argued a lot. My father was a Sunday school teacher, but he was a bear at home."

"How did he treat you, Cheryl?"

Cheryl's head dropped slowly. "Okay, I guess."

"How did he show you that he loved you?"

"He didn't!" She exploded: "He doesn't love me. He always teased me and picked on me or let my brothers pick on me."

"How do you relate to him now?"

"As little as possible. I stay away from home unless I absolutely have to go there. When I do go, I stay for only a day or two. I can't stand any more than that."

Cheryl's difficulties were painfully obvious. Her parents had not communicated love and acceptance to her. They hadn't given her the freedom to fail when she was a child, so she withdrew from them, unwilling to risk possible rejection.

Cheryl's relationship with God mirrored her relationship with her parents. She felt that she could never do enough to please the Lord, and yet she felt guilty if she didn't try to serve Him. Her parents' belittling led her to feel God was doing the same. She had begun to belittle herself and to fear relating to anyone.

In addition, Cheryl thought about herself almost all the time. *Have I done enough today? What did my boss think of me when I said that? I wonder if I should have said no to Bill? Why do I feel this way? There must be something wrong with me!* Cheryl's introspection was morbid and paralyzing. Her immobility created tremendous guilt because she knew that God wanted her to be obedient to Him. She knew what she should do, but fear of rejection prevented her from doing it. Then she also felt guilty. As motivators for behavior, fear and guilt are a fairly lethal combination!

Unaffectionate Parents

If you met Susan on the street, you might think that she sang in her church choir. In reality, she has slept with three different men this past week alone, and has been with twelve others over the past month. How did she get into such a lifestyle? Her problem started a long time ago.

At the age of eight, Susan said to herself, *There must be something wrong with me. My Daddy won't hug me or touch me, or spend time with me. I guess I'm not what I ought to be. If I were, Daddy would love me!*

Her father was a decent man, but he had grown up in a non-touching home. Such children, as they mature, will tend to see physical affection only as a part of sexual activity. They will tend to be non-touchers as fathers, much to the detriment of their children.

By the time Susan was thirteen, she was trying to find the love from other men that her father had withheld from her. Her promiscuity caused her to be "popular" with older boys, even with older men.

She got married, but not because she deeply loved her husband. She married to get the affection she had always wanted but had never received from her father. As you can imagine, the couple had serious problems. After a while, one man couldn't meet Susan's insatiable desire for affection. There wasn't a chance for her marriage to succeed!

Susan realized something was wrong within her, but she couldn't pinpoint what it was. It was as though she looked through a window at her own conduct, was shocked by it, and yet was unable to change it. She stumbled through life confused, hurting, and acting out her craving for fatherly love. Only through hours of counseling did Susan recognize her real problem. She was still a little girl, just trying to get her Daddy to love her.

Not only did Susan struggle with how she felt about herself and in her other relationships, she had a very difficult time relying on God. It was almost inconceivable to her that God could really comfort her or meet her emotional needs. Susan's situation typifies a relatively predictable phenomenon which we call "the absent-father syndrome."

The Absent-Father Syndrome

The absent-father-syndrome is present in a large percentage of American homes. It is not a sickness, but a social disease which robs fathers of the enjoyment that should be theirs. Its effects are usually lifelong in duration, and are sometimes devastating for the children.

The syndrome occurs when the father is absent from the home due to death, divorce, prolonged withdrawal, or disinterest. The result is that he doesn't provide his children with the time and emotional support they need. Perhaps this is because he simply doesn't know how. Maybe his father didn't provide those needs for him. Or, perhaps problems between his wife and himself are preventing him from offering his children their emotional requirements.

The father may perceive of the home as his wife's domain. Rather than providing any real input there, he withdraws to other activities (e.g., business, sports, the church) which enable him to feel more successful. In some cases, the climate may be more pleasant elsewhere. He reasons that he doesn't need the static; he doesn't need the criticism; and home is where he gets both.

Some fathers, after a divorce, feel it's no longer their place to act as "father." But, for whatever reason, he's absent from his child's life, and the child is the big loser. Nobody will be able to take the father's place.

There are usually four effects on the daughter: First, she will reject her appearance and sometimes even her femininity. If she could not attract her father, then who would ever be attracted to her? She will always feel at a disadvantage, no matter how attractive she might be. Second, she will crave attention and affection. She will love being held and will never seem to get enough. This may leave her vulnerable to becoming sexually active with some young man, who will gladly exchange embraces for other pleasures. Many a father has been astounded to learn of his daughter's sexual activities, when in actuality he set her up for them. The exception to this is the woman who resents all men so deeply that she desires no attention from men whatsoever. Third, she will be a "rejection sponge." The smallest inconsistency in her husband or friends will be taken as out-and-out rejection. She may not understand how someone could ever love her. This rejection sensitivity will not be linked to just her husband, but will have its influence in all her relationships. Fourth, she will find herself attracted to older men, looking for a "dad," and she may marry an older man. This can often result in sexual dysfunction in the marriage, as she finds herself unable to "sleep with dad." Also, since her father was a passive figure, she may find herself attracted to passive men.

Most importantly, a woman who is a product of the absent-father syndrome will find it difficult to trust God. The association of who a father is was made early, and she may experience a great deal of insecurity and aloneness, as she is unable to trust even God the Father.

Sons also are affected by the absent-father syndrome. They have lost their male role model, and so they either depend on their mother or are forced to look out into the world for a role model. In looking to the world, they will often desire to become the "macho-man," which is usually just an act to hide insecurity in not being able to identify with men. If they look to the mother as the role model, it can lead to a loss of masculinity. Like the daughters, the sons also find themselves craving masculine attention and affection, which can cause vulnerability to homosexual interaction. They will mistake sex for love, and like the daughters, become rejection sponges. Since mother was the dominant figure in the home, they will also have great difficulty trusting the Heavenly Father.

So what can be done? Fathers, accept your responsibility to be a father. Spend time with your children. Love is spelled T - I - M - E. Everything else you provide them is junk, if you don't provide love first.

Wives, give your husbands the opportunities to be active in the home. Release control and risk his making mistakes in parenting. Lovingly support him in his part of disciplining and decision-making.

Above all, do everything in your power as parents to keep your marriage intact. If marital difficulties have you considering divorce, seek professional help.

Daughter or son, your solution is not in blaming, but in forgiving your father. If you don't forgive, his mistakes will haunt you for the rest of your life. Blaming never helps change things. [1]

Emotionally Distant, Inactive Parents

Withdrawal sometimes occurs when a parent feels overwhelmed by life's pressures and activities. Children feel abandoned. Young children usually believe it must be their fault. This perception is often confirmed by the withdrawing parent who, also feeling guilty for not being a loving and responsible parent, blames the child.

As the child enters other relationships, he always holds back. He wants to protect himself from being abandoned again, yet his lack of commitment ultimately damages the relationship. This kind of "protection" actually results in more pain and a lack of intimacy in relationships.

It is also hard for these people to accept love. They could not provoke the love of their parents, so there must be something really wrong with them. They resist accepting another's love at face value. They feel lonely, guilty, and condemned.

Finally, when it comes to God, they see Him as distant and uninvolved. They hear of others' vibrant relationships with God and determine that God isn't like that to them because they're such poor Christians.

Abusive Parents

Patricia volunteered to serve in a Christian organization. During her orientation, a speaker gave a series of lectures entitled, "God, Our Father."

Every time his lectures began, Patricia would get up and leave the room. She had a problem! Her relationship with her father had been the opposite of what Susan (in the first case study) had experienced. Patricia's father had constantly molested and humiliated her during her childhood. She lived in constant dread of his presence in the home, particularly at night. She was afraid to tell her mother what was taking place. Consequently, Patricia lived in lonely, silent fear. Her childhood was nothing more than a living hell.

She couldn't bear the suggestion that God was like a "father" to her! The category for the word "father," shaped by her relationship with her dad, was too vile to be applied to God. As a result, she didn't have a positive concept of God as Father, and the very mention of it created trauma within her.

She became physically ill during the lectures, and would have to go to bed. She explained to a friend, "I don't want a relationship with God the Father. I have one with Jesus, and that's enough for me!"

Since Patricia could not trust her own father, what sort of a relationship could she establish with her Heavenly Father? For her, worship of God was impersonal. There could be no emotion, no affection, no trust between her and God the Father.

Strange as it may seem, the reason she had chosen to enter a Christian vocation was directly related to her problem. You see, thinking of God as a person, a friend, was not possible for her. She followed a cold and impersonal set of rules, and she sought to relate to God by "serving" Him. She wanted to appease Him by sacrificially living as His volunteer in a religious organization. Intimate times of prayer with Him were impossible. The best she could attempt was to read from devotional books.

A young child who is abused will believe that something must be wrong with himself. His reasoning is that even though his parent was wrong, he must have somehow provoked the situation. The shame is overwhelming, and his ability to relate to others is severely disturbed.

Perfectionistic Parents

Perfectionistic people may make great employees, but they're lousy parents unless they change their natural responses to their children. Their standards are so high and rigid that even they cannot attain them. Neither can their children.

It is shattering for a child to feel that he can never measure up in his parents' eyes. Often, the parents rationalize that they are only pushing their child so that he might experience the most out of life, but they may be pushing him over the emotional edge. The child will feel he cannot measure up. Some will try desperately, often fighting the depression of repressed hurt and anger later in life. The others may simply rebel. Rebellious children often have perfectionistic parents. The child may also avoid relating to peers who succeed. He will tend to run instead with those who are failures and aren't threatening to him.

Whether they rebel or try to play the perfectionist game, these children struggle in their perception of God. They just can never do enough for Him. Sometimes they participate in ritualistic church activities. Sometimes they drop out completely. In either case, they feel distant and condemned by God.

Objectivity and Loyalty

Some people feel guilty when they begin to evaluate a parent's lifestyles and influence. It's as though they were becoming disloyal, unloving children. That's just not the case! Taking an honest look at your heritage does not mean you must respond with vindictiveness or harshly judge your father and mother. It simply means you recognize that they gave you the best they could give at the time! Whether their parenting was good or bad, they tried their best.

Be benevolent as you think about the way they raised you! At the same time, you must become the generation where the further passage of these negative consequences is ended. In order to accomplish that, you must become objective and understand what has taken place in your family.

Your story is being written as you read these pages! What will it be like? For Susan and Patricia, there was the record of confusion, pain, and struggle. You have the God-given opportunity to choose for yourself what your life will be like. The process may be painful and difficult, but change is possible. As we continue, think about what your life would be like if it were included in this chapter!

[1]Jim Craddock, "The Absent-Father Syndrome" (Houston, TX: Rapha Publishing, 1986).

Three

LOOKIN' FOR LOVE

The true stories in Chapter Two all demonstrate the powerful influence relationships have on us. Relationships, and especially our relationship with God, are the key to life. They are our foundation of stability and fulfillment. But those who have not experienced love and affirmation often turn to other ways of finding stability and fulfillment: success and possessions. These other ways, however, don't work. No matter how hard we try, they cannot replace meaningful relationships.

What do these counterfeit goals look like? Here are a few quotes:

"The good life is successfully achieving your goals."
"It means you have plenty of money to do what you wish."
"A quality life requires you to have a good job, a good
spouse, and good health."
"The best life? It begins when you have freedom to take long
vacations, own your own business, live in a beautiful home,
and drive expensive cars."

According to John 8:44, Satan is the father of lies; his goal is to make us believe his lies. One of the greatest myths he tells us is that our success and possessions determine the quality of life we will experience. But that's simply not true. God has made us in such a way that success, pleasure, and possessions cannot ultimately satisfy us. Relationships (and especially our relationship with Him) provide our real fulfillment. Some of us may be more goal-oriented than others, but we are all "lookin' for love."

Sarah: Enriched by Love

Sarah's father was a tailor, and her mother was a Swedish immigrant. Her father had no money when the couple married in 1923. He worked eighteen-hour days to create enough savings to invest in his own business. In 1927, he finally reached his objective. He prospered, bought a home, and had several employees. Then, in 1931, the Great Depression wiped him out. There were no more rich men to buy his finely tailored suits. He had an emotional breakdown, unable to cope with the loss of all he had worked to create.

Sarah remembers her father during that bleak period. He slept on the couch while she tiptoed around the house, playing quietly with her dolls. She vividly remembers how their fine home was lost in a foreclosure and auctioned off for a fraction of what it had cost to build it. They moved to a tiny apartment–and then another–and another.

But there was love in that family, no matter where they had to live! Sarah's two older brothers and mother constantly showed her affection. Even Sarah's father emerged from his self-pity and became very affirming of her. While she recognized that their food had become very plain, there was always enough to go around. Her brothers whooped and shouted as they played with their little sister in the alleyway. There was always a lengthy family time after the evening meal, with open communication and laughter. Sarah particularly looked forward to the honest interaction that took place among the family members then.

Sarah learned to love God in a poverty-filled house. Their finances had nothing to do with the amount of faith and trust in God which existed in her home. Love isn't expensive! Its value can't be weighed using the same scale for gold.

Today, Sarah is the wife of a pastor and the mother of three sons. Her oldest brother is the president of a seminary and her other brother is a missionary reaching teenagers in France. Her father died penniless, but he has enriched the world through introducing his three children to the Lord.

Eric: Material Wealth and Emotional Poverty

Eric was the product of a night of passion between a couple who enjoyed living on the fast track. They didn't want children, and they accepted his presence with thinly-veiled resentment.

His father was an attorney, his mother a designer. Their millions had been inherited. Their posh residences in New York and Palm Beach were designed for throwing parties.

During Eric's childhood, his parents shouted at him: "Don't touch that!" "Leave it alone!" "Be careful!" Each room was filled with expensive and fragile antiques that created endless reasons for him to feel out of place. He was severely beaten by his father when he was only three years old for damaging a treasured vase. He was constantly reminded of his own worthlessness and the high value of things.

Eric's parents seldom told him they loved him. They rarely hugged him or encouraged him in his studies or sports. His "nannies" came and went, some trying harder than others to befriend him.

He still remembers the night he deliberately snapped off the hood ornament of his father's favorite Rolls Royce. He was eight years old at the time. He later said, "I enjoyed the beating I got. It was worth every bit of it to see his rage over that stupid thing being broken."

Eric became increasingly destructive. On one occasion, he deliberately poured black paint on his parents' expensive Persian rugs. His mother sent him to a psychiatrist to get help with "his problem."

He spent his school years in private boarding schools, dreading holidays and vacation periods. When he was eighteen, he left the United States to roam around Europe. He sank into the drug scene, became evasive and withdrawn, and spent several months in prison cells.

When he was thirty years old, he encountered his first Christians in a free clinic on London's east side. It took several weeks before a trust relationship developed between Eric and the workers there. Finally, Eric said, "My parents always told me that they didn't want a child. The last words I ever heard from my mother's lips were another reminder that I was an accident. I never want to see them again as long as I live."

Relationships Make the Difference

If a child is born into a family where affirmation and love are bountifully provided, he or she will probably develop a healthy self-image. If the family gives affirmation as a reward for success, and love becomes a reward for behaving properly, the child will develop an insecure, competitive spirit. In each case, the child is shaped by the relationships within his or her home.

How does alcoholism affect the shaping of a child? What is the impact of a mother who didn't want her child? What happens to a child thrust into a school room with a neurotic teacher who ridicules his every mistake? What is the consequence of placing a teen in a drug-infested school, where violence in the hallways is a common occurrence?

A fractured childhood produces a variety of painful results. In some people, it produces a fire so strong, so overpowering, that they experience intense guilt, anger, and bitterness. They are driven to succeed to prove their worth, and are often thwarted in their close associations with others because they haven't been able to experience warm, affirming relationships.

Others have a different defense mechanism. Instead of being driven to succeed, they try to avoid the pain of rejection and failure by withdrawing from risks–socially, professionally, and every other way.

Many of us are a combination of these two extremes. We are driven to succeed in those relationships and tasks where we are likely to do well, but we become passive when the risks seem to be too great.

A few tortured souls leave family and friends behind in the hope of finding love and acceptance. It is a miserable search when they take the wrong path.

On the Edge of Disaster

For example, the wife of a missionary and mother of three small children came to her counselor and declared, "God has told me to leave my husband and marry another person!" This young wife had been a committed Christian, who, up to this point, had seemed totally devoted to her husband and calling. What was it that made her willing to give up everything for another man?

She explained that this man had become her closest friend; that they could talk about anything and pray about everything together, and that life with him was an adventure she had never experienced with her spouse.

During counseling sessions, several things stood out. She felt just as committed to Christ as she had before the affair began, and she also did not view her third-party involvement as being either sinful or immoral.

The counselor learned that her father had left the family when she was still a small child and that she had never established a relationship with her stepfather. She married her husband not because of her deep love for him, but because she felt "he would be good for her." In fact, she had been far more infatuated with another man prior to marrying her husband.

Problems of adjustment started immediately after the wedding. Instead of getting better, their problems grew worse. She felt frustrated, angry, disillusioned. *Surely*, she thought, *marriage should be better than this.*

To her, it seemed as though her husband centered on their physical relationship. He always wanted to make love–"as though that would make everything right."

A strange feeling began to emerge within her. She tried to be a dutiful wife, but feelings of revulsion toward sex grew stronger. As she described her feelings toward her husband to her counselor, he recognized that these same words were used by little girls to describe sexually abusive fathers or stepfathers.

This woman was trying to make her husband meet her longing for a father's love. Her husband became confused and angry. Rather than admit that his marriage was failing, he tried to promote his masculinity by being sexually aggressive. This only increased the tension between them.

Then she met a man at church who treated her like a lady. She was instantly attracted to him, although he was almost fifteen years her senior. He not only showed her the attention and consideration she was seeking, but was understanding and sympathetic as well.

They started the relationship by just talking. Soon, she was sharing her frustration and sadness with him, and he was confiding in her about his problems with his wife. Of course, as he understood her problems, she understood his. It felt so good just to be held...

Through loving confrontation, time, and a responsive heart, God worked in this woman, and her marriage was saved. The Heavenly Father restored the marriage and ministry she had beside her husband–but they nearly fell as victims of the damage which had been done to her by her father.

Parental relationships, more than any other factor, create the quality of life we experience as adults. Someone has said, "You will be the same person five years from now that you are today, except for one thing: the people you meet." We might add, "You are today the product of the people you have spent time with, especially your parents."

Divorce and Children

Consider the impact made upon a child in a home where divorce fractures the normal flow of life. Here is the true account of one victim. She said: "I grew up in a relatively happy, secure home. We lived in a lush, green valley in the middle of Washington State, with an icy-cold, mountain river running through it. I had a really great childhood!

"Then I hit adolescence–that horrible time when you don't know if you're a child or an adult. It's an identity-building time. In the seventh grade, I was chosen to be an honor student. But in the eighth grade, I was flunking out!"

What could have happened to cause such a turnaround in a young girl? In this case, it was a hungry, vicious, social disease that's eating away at many families today. It's called divorce.

According to this young woman: "I never saw my parents fight. Later, I learned that this lack of fighting was their basic problem. They couldn't fight because they couldn't communicate at all. As the wall of bitterness grew, it became more impossible to overcome the problems in our home, and my parents' relationship became barren and empty. If only I could have seen what was going to happen.

"I vividly remember the day they told me they were going to get a divorce," she said. "It seemed like the only logical solution to them.

I don't think they realized it would become an open sore that would never completely heal within me. There had been no warning, no fights, no screaming and yelling. I remember my heart pounding as sickening fear consumed me. It was like sitting in a car with no brakes, rolling toward a cliff, going faster and faster.

"At fourteen, just after the divorce, I began to make my own rules," she said. (Guilt-ridden parents often find it difficult to impose discipline, especially after a painful divorce.) "My anger and rebellion grew. I was a walking time bomb, filled with anger that would go off at the slightest bump.

"I chose friends who were also hurting and angry. I partied, drank, smoked, cussed, skipped school, harassed the teachers and police, shoplifted, and much more...."

The fracturing of the relationship between her parents indelibly marked this girl's life. For all of us, relationships create our quality of life–healthy or unhealthy, bitter or sweet, secure or confused.

Biblical Examples and Admonition to Parents

In ancient Israel, a father's first responsibility was to guide his son. This awareness saturated the Jewish culture. The book of Proverbs contains potent chapters of teachings shared by King Solomon with his son. In praise of God, the prophet Isaiah wrote "...fathers tell their children about your faithfulness." (Is. 38:19) Think about that statement. How else could a child know about God's faithfulness if parents had not experienced it and then shared it?

In Deuteronomy, Moses talked to Israel's fathers about their earlier deliverance from Pharaoh's army at the Red Sea. He reminded them that their children were not present, and insisted they must share this experience of God's faithfulness. He says in 11:18-21:

Fix these words of mine in your hearts and minds; tie them as symbols on your hands and bind them on your foreheads. Teach them to your children, talking about them when you sit at home and when you walk along the road, when you lie down and when you get up. Write them on the doorframes of your houses and on your gates, so that your days and the days of your children may be many in the land that the Lord swore to give your forefathers, as many as the days that the heavens are above the earth.

Nothing has changed! A child's development in all areas—social, intellectual, physical, emotional, spiritual—is still the responsibility of the father and the mother. When parents offer a healthy balance of love and discipline, they produce healthy, well-balanced young adults. But when parents are unattached to God and relate poorly to their offspring, they create much pain and sadness for them.

Relationships Provide Our Role Models

From the first day of life, we pattern our actions after people who are close to us. Children instinctively copy the attitudes and actions of those they are exposed to most. It is God's design that they copy loving and protective parents, but many parents don't cooperate in this plan.

Recently, a parent gave her three-year-old child a science fiction video movie to occupy him while she pursued her own interests. Unattended, the youngster watched it seven times.

In the movie, a man with a patch over one eye rode a motorcycle while killing and maiming others at the rate of several per minute. The child later went into his bedroom and improvised a costume like the one worn by the man in the movie. He then began riding his tricycle around the neighborhood, a patch over one eye, viciously clobbering with a baseball bat all the little kids he met. Several were badly cut or bruised.

This child was simply copying his role model. He didn't have enough judgment to select a worthy model, so he copied what his own mother had endorsed when she gave him a videotape as an electronic baby sitter.

Just as unwittingly, we also unconsciously pattern ourselves after our role models, whether good or bad. Husbands who batter their wives almost invariably have come from homes where violence was commonplace. A loving and gregarious person usually comes from a secure, loving home environment.

We become like the person we are exposed to the most, even if that person is cruel toward us. Our role models have powerful effects on us.

Positive role models provide powerfully positive results. Have you ever met a couple who has been happily married for years and now even look like they are brother and sister? Or, have you ever met a young man who walked, talked, and spoke like an older person he admired?

How about you? Who is the model for your life? How powerfully has this individual influenced you? Do you talk, walk, think, and reflect this person in your own mannerisms? What are you like today because of your father, your mother, or the lack of one of them? We pick up our life patterns without thought, selecting from this person and that one ways to deal with life. Seldom is any of it intentional. It just–happens.

Four

EMPTY SOLUTIONS

If a person has received affirmation, encouragement, protection, loving discipline, and time from his parents, then he will probably feel confident and secure as an adult. He will be able to relate well to the Lord and to other people. He will be willing to try new things, take chances, and even laugh at his mistakes.

Emotional, spiritual, and relational health is more or less proportional to the degree of love and positive modeling a person experiences. If a person has not experienced loving and strong parental modeling, then there will be a vacuum in his life. Virtually everything he does will be designed to accomplish two purposes: to gain the approval he so desperately wants, and to avoid pain. We come up with all kinds of ways to win approval and avoid pain. They seem like good solutions, but there's one problem with them: ultimately, they don't work. Let's examine a few of these alluring, but empty alternative solutions.

Looking for a White Knight

If I only had James (or whomever), *then I'd be really happy!* Some of us are waiting for someone to gallop into our lives on a handsome horse (or a new red Camaro!) and give us the attention and affection we want. We may be waiting for a spouse or a friend to meet our deepest needs and make us really happy. Occasionally, someone comes along who seems to be "that special person." Our expectations (and demands) are sky-high, but sooner or later, that person falls off his horse and we drop him like a lead balloon. Then we look for someone else to make us happy.

Many marriages begin this way. One partner expects the other to provide happiness, contentment, and excitement. After a few weeks, a few months, or a few years, these unrealistic expectations are shattered, and the couple gets divorced so they can look for someone else to make them happy.

The Ostrich Syndrome

All of us have some kind of defense mechanism, but some of us have taken these mechanisms to an extreme. Like the proverbial ostrich with his head in the sand (ostriches don't really do that, you know!), we escape from reality by withdrawing, denying the truth in our lives, becoming passive, indecisive, and numb. The desire to avoid pain has a very negative consequence, however. When we block out pain in this way, we also block out intimacy, warmth, and affection. When we avoid the pain of rejection, we also avoid the pleasure of relationships.

This denial leads to either of two seemingly unrelated responses. Some people get clinically depressed as they suppress their pain and anger. Others, conversely, become idealistic, and say that everything is "just fine" and "getting better" without objectively seeing the good, the bad, and the ugly in life. That objectivity is just too painful; so, they hide behind their idealism.

The "Rambo" Defense

Some people see others in one of two groups: *for me or against me.* Those who are for them can do no wrong, but those who disagree with them are branded as terrible, awful people. The latter are attacked for being stupid, narrow, mean, or whatever epithet comes out.

These "Rambo" attacks are not reserved entirely for others, however. People like this sometimes reserve their harshest attacks for themselves. They call themselves horrible names and berate themselves terribly. This anger is a form of self-hatred.

The 007 Technique

Some of us attack openly, but some attack in secret behind another's back. These people covertly get others on their side, forming alliances and turning people against the object(s) of their scorn. Gossip is the main weapon used to secretly condemn others and elevate ourselves. It is an insidious and deadly practice.

Rat on a Treadmill

Most of us are driven people, racing to accomplish goals, trying to succeed, getting attention, and avoiding any reflection on the emptiness in our lives. We are busy from the moment we get up until we go to bed. Even our devotional lives (if we have one) are characterized by this frantic pace. We read this chapter or that one, pray through our list, close our Bibles, check it off our "to do" list, and continue racing through our day.

Mary and Martha characterize the contrast between a reflective and a driven person. Jesus went to visit these women, and Mary...

> ...was listening to the Lord's word, seated at His feet. But Martha was distracted with all her preparations; and she came up to Him, and said, "Lord, do You not care that my sister has left me to do all the serving alone? Then tell her to help me." But the Lord answered and said to her, "Martha, Martha, you are worried and bothered about so many things; but only a few things are necessary, really only one, for Mary has chosen the good part, which shall not be taken away from her."
>
> Luke 10:39-42

Many of us are obsessive-compulsive: obsessed with thinking about all we "have to do" and compulsively driven to get it all done. We are like rats on a treadmill, always running but never getting very far.

Puppets

In both function and purpose, many of us are puppets who do whatever others want us to do, say what they want us to say, and be what they want us to be. Our purpose is to please others, to impress them, and to perform well enough to win their approval.

Some of us have a finely tuned sense of perception. We are able to sense how our words, actions, attitudes, and tone of voice will affect others. Then we change our behavior to please them. We are puppets who respond to every pull on our emotional strings.

Escapists

The pain from relationships leads many people to the numbing effects of alcohol and drugs. The reason these chemicals are used is because they are effective and reliable, if only for a short time. The fact that someone would use this method to numb himself, while being aware of the chemical's destructiveness, can only demonstrate how desperate a person may be to end his pain. The use of drugs only compounds the problem, adding another layer of "protection" that keeps him from seeing and dealing with reality in his life.

Most people are some combination of several of these empty solutions. We orchestrate our lives for two purposes: to win approval and avoid pain. But no matter how hard we try, we experience only limited relief from the gnawing fear and pain of rejection and failure.

We need to see the truth. Reality may be painful, but it is the only way to see growth and health in our lives. The other alternatives are not cute. They aren't clever. They are seductive and pathological. They rob us of intimacy, strength, and hope. The sooner we begin to realize the emptiness of these alternatives, the sooner we will begin to experience the refreshment of God's truth, God's Spirit, and God's people.

SECTION II

THE SOLUTION: Accurately Perceiving God and Yourself

Five

LET GOD BE YOUR MODEL

If we could go through a second childhood, if we could relate to someone who is consistently accepting and loving, we could be healed from the damage of our childhood. But can we? We not only *can*, but this is exactly what *should* take place beginning at the point of our salvation. We are born again, with a new Father, who loves and cares for us completely. And we enter a family that can provide warmth, affirmation, encouragement, and hope.

For some of us, our parents have modeled the love and strength of God very consistently. But for many of us, the criticism, abuse, neglect, or demands of our parents have produced painful emotions and destructive habits in our lives. No matter how badly your parents modeled the character of God, you can have hope for health, strength, and intimacy. God has given us the truth of His word, the power of His Spirit, and the warmth and encouragement of His people so that our self-concepts, relationships with Him, and our relationships with others can be changed. These solutions aren't based on pop psychology. They are based on the timeless truths of the Scriptures and the eternal nature of a loving and powerful God. He is a kind and patient Father who wants to show His love to His children.

Let God Be Your Model

Is it possible to choose your role model; to choose the one you emulate? Is it possible to pattern your life after someone who is infinitely loving, protecting, and giving?

Yes! It is possible, but it doesn't happen by pressing a button. You don't rid yourself of twenty, thirty, forty, or fifty years of an inferior role model in an instant. It takes understanding, perception, endurance...and guts!

We need to start with a clear understanding of the character of God and the lies of Satan. The Lord has said, "Taste of Me, and see that I am good." He is a wonderful Father. He is patient, kind and loving, not envious, not boastful, not arrogant nor rude. He is never self-seeking. He is not quick to take offense. He keeps no score of wrongs. He does not gloat over men's sins. He knows no limit to His endurance, and no end to His trust.

Perhaps you are thinking, *That's hard to consider as an option. I don't know Him well enough to know if I can be like Him, or even if I want to be like Him. And He is not tangible. How can I know what He's really like?*

Don't Let Satan Blind You to the Reality of God's Character

Have you been blinded by Satan to the reality of God's character? He has three objectives in your life:

1. *He wants to distort the character of God.*
2. *He wants you to believe that your relationship with the Lord is conditional and based on how good you can be.*
3. *He wants you to depend on another person for your security and significance instead of depending on God.*

Satan distorts our view of the character of God. By doing so, he isolates us from His help, His strength, and His love. Has he done this to you?

Here's a test: who do you turn to first when you have a problem? Is it God? Or, is it only when all else fails that you will then turn to the Father for help?

When our view of God is not right, we are left in charge of our own lives. We see ourselves as the victims of our circumstances, thus we are more easily tormented by our failures and sins. If Satan can cause you pain and then make you associate it with the Father, he has succeeded in eroding your perception of a loving and powerful God.

Most of us have a faulty view of God as Father. We haven't based our concept of God the Father on the inspired Word of God. Our concept is based on our relationships with our earthly fathers.

To a great host of believers, the heavenly Father is a vague spiritual being, a cosmic policeman ten million light-years away. For all practical purposes, God the Father is a stranger. And we don't trust strangers, much less love them. How can we put any confidence in One we hardly know? The answer is, we can't!

There's a clear connection between our knowledge of God and our emotional distresses. James 1:6 describes the consequences of not being able to trust God: *"...for the one who doubts is like the surf of the sea driven and tossed by the wind."*

We tend to ascribe to God the characteristics of our fathers: good or bad, loving or cruel, protective or passive, gentle or aloof, etc. Some of us, therefore, have a very positive picture of God because our fathers modeled the love and strength of God to a large degree. But some of us have a very poor view of God because our fathers presented a harsh or passive model.

How can our belief system be changed? The answer to this dilemma lies in the character of Jesus Christ. He has shown us the Father.

In John 14:8-13 we read:

> *Philip said, "Lord, show us the Father and that will be enough for us." Jesus answered: "Don't you know me, Philip, even after I have been among you such a long time? Anyone who has seen me has seen the Father. How can you say, 'Show us the Father'? Don't you believe that I am in the Father, and that the Father is in me? The words I say to you are not just my own. Rather, it is the Father, living in me, who is doing his work. Believe me when I say that I am in the Father and the Father is in me; or at least believe on the evidence of the miracles themselves. I tell you the truth, anyone who has faith in me will do what I have been doing. He will*

> *do even greater things than these, because I am going to the*
> *Father. And I will do whatever you ask in my name, so that the*
> *Son may bring glory to the Father."*

Even though the disciples had been with Jesus continually for three years, some of them seemed surprised to discover that Jesus was God. They had not really understood that. Similarly, it is amazing that we really don't understand that Jesus, the Father, and the Holy Spirit are different persons yet one essence.

All Jesus did, all He said, all the miracles He performed demonstrated His unity with the Father. The Father revealed Himself to us in the life, death, and resurrection of Christ.

Time and time again, Jesus reiterated this important truth. Here are some passages that describe the unity of the Father and the Son. Examine each one carefully:

> *Jesus gave them this answer: "I tell you the truth, the Son can do*
> *nothing by himself; he can do only what he sees his Father doing,*
> *because whatever the Father does the Son also does. For the*
> *Father loves the Son and shows him all he does. Yes, to your*
> *amazement he will show him even greater things than these. For*
> *just as the Father raises the dead and gives them life, even so the*
> *Son gives life to whom he is pleased to give it. Moreover, the*
> *Father judges no one, but has entrusted all judgment to the Son,*
> *that all may honor the Son just as they honor the Father. He who*
> *does not honor the Son does not honor the Father, who sent him. I*
> *tell you the truth, whoever hears my word and believes him who*
> *sent me has eternal life and will not be condemned; he has crossed*
> *over from death to life. I tell you the truth, a time is coming and*
> *has now come when the dead will hear the voice of the Son of God*
> *and those who hear will live. For as the Father has life in himself,*
> *so he has granted the Son to have life in himself. And he has given*
> *him authority to judge because he is the Son of Man."*
>
> John 5:19-27

*I am one who testifies for myself; my other witness is the Father,
who sent me.* John 8:18

*The one who sent me is with me; he has not left me alone, for I
always do what pleases him.* John 8:29

*Jesus said to them, "If God were your Father, you would love me,
for I came from God and now am here. I have not come on my
own; but he sent me."* John 8:42

*"I tell you the truth," Jesus answered, "before Abraham was born,
I am!"* John 8:58

I and the Father are one. John 10:30

*"Do not let your hearts be troubled. Trust in God; trust also in me.
In my Father's house are many rooms; if it were not so, I would
have told you. I am going there to prepare a place for you. And if I
go and prepare a place for you, I will come back and take you to
be with me that you also may be where I am. You know the way to
the place where I am going." Thomas said to him, "Lord, we don't
know where you are going, so how can we know the way?" Jesus
answered, "I am the way and the truth and the life. No one comes
to the Father except through me. If you really knew me, you would
know my Father as well. From now on, you do know him and have
seen him."* John 14:1-7

The Father, the Son, and the Holy Spirit are one. God the Son stepped out of heaven and became a man so that God's love, forgiveness, and care would be demonstrated in person to heal and comfort those who were so desperately hurting.

We must learn to see the Father in the character, words, and actions of Jesus. The Holy Spirit will then begin to change our erroneous concepts of the Father into correct ones, with all of the accompanying benefits. Do you think God the Father would treat you differently than

Jesus would? No! The way Jesus acted is exactly like the Heavenly Father.

We tend to think God is so huge and impersonal that He doesn't feel pain. But He does! Christ endured the excruciating pain of being beaten, whipped, and nailed to the cross. He endured the emotional pain of being deserted by His friends, spat on by His enemies, and jeered at by the crowds who had hailed Him as King only days earlier. And He endured the humanly unimaginable, spiritual pain of taking on Himself the punishment for every sin ever committed, and being separated from the Father for the first and only time in eternity so that the righteous wrath of God could be poured out on Him who had known no sin. As the hymn writer expressed it:

> *Amazing love, how can it be*
> *That Christ my God should die for me?* [1]

Because you were not forced to die in such a way, don't take His death for granted. Don't forget what the cross says to us about the Father's amazing love, demonstrated by Jesus' sacrificial death!

What did Christ's death accomplish for us? His sacrificial death paid fully for our sins which separated us from God. His atonement justified us–that is, it made us right in His sight. His death propitiated, or averted, the righteous wrath of God toward us. And among other incredible truths, His payment for our sins enabled us to be adopted as children of God. These two Scriptural passages explain our adoption:

> *But when the time had fully come, God sent his Son, born of a woman, born under law, to redeem those under law, that we might receive the full rights of sons. Because you are sons, God sent the Spirit of his Son into our hearts, the Spirit who calls out, "Abba, Father." So you are no longer a slave, but a son; and since you are a son, God has made you also an heir.*
>
> Gal. 4:4-7

For you did not receive a spirit that makes you a slave again to fear, but you received the Spirit of sonship. And by him we cry, "Abba, Father."   Rom. 8:15

No matter how well or how poorly our fathers modeled the character of God, we can be convinced of our Heavenly Father's love and power. Certainly it is to our advantage to have had a good model in our parents, but for those of us who didn't, we have the clear and strong teaching of God's word, the working of God's Spirit, and the encouragement of God's people to help us understand.

As we recognize how we have been deceived as to who God is, it will be helpful to consider what it means to *become as a child so that we might truly know Him* (Matt. 18:2-3).

What does this mean? Consider these aspects of the parent-child relationship:

- A child gains a sense of security based on the trust he has in his parents.

- The child looks to the parents to see if they're calm in times of trouble. If the child believes the parents are upset, he too, will soon become upset.

- The child feels he will be okay if he just obeys his parents' instructions.

- The child "knows" everything will be okay as long as his parents give forth a confident assurance of such.

- The child feels special because he is so special to his parents.

- The child can be happy even if he/she doesn't know everything that is going on. Then the child is able to relax and enjoy life.

- The child will not tolerate bad thoughts toward his parents.

- The child likes being around his parents.

There are really two focuses in our search to know God as Father. One is cognitive. God has taken great care to describe Himself to us. He did so in order that we might compare what we were thinking about Him to what He says about Himself. We must put aside that which is false and put on the truth. As important as this is, there is also an experiential part. We must actively choose to become a child to the heavenly Father. He says *"taste of Me and see that I am good."* If we release ourselves from believing lies about Him, and allow Him to Father us again, we will find the freedom He intends for us. The rest of this book is designed to lead you to this truth. But there is one thing you have to do before you start. You must choose to give up your former solutions and instead choose only Him. This will not be a one-time choice, but one you will have to make each day...sometimes each hour.

As you read, pray that God will reveal to you which beliefs you have about Him that are wrong and how you can experience being His child more fully.

[1]John Newton, "Amazing Grace," stanzas 1-4, 1779. Tune by Virginia Harmony, 1831. Arranged by Edwin O. Excell, 1900. Source: *The Baptist Hymnal* (Nashville, TN: Convention Press), 1975 ed.

Six

GOD WANTS US TO KNOW HIM
AS FATHER

Some friends of ours, who had tried for years to have a baby, have recently adopted a child. The little boy was only three days old when they took him home from the hospital, and though this couple only had a few days notice from the adoption agency, they were thrilled beyond words! Their love for this adopted infant couldn't have been stronger if he had been their own flesh and blood.

We have been adopted, too. The Scriptures teach us that we have been adopted by God into His family, but our adoption isn't quite like the one I just described. We didn't come to God with a virtually blank slate like an infant. Much of our emotional and relational grid was firmly in place when we became Christians.

An illustration that better describes our situation is the story of a couple in Iowa who has adopted a houseful of children between the ages of five and twelve. These children were all deeply hurt by neglect, abuse, or the sudden loss of both parents. Nobody else wanted these misfits, these "problem children," but the Iowa couple took them into their home and adopted them. A few of them had more emotional stability than others, and they responded relatively quickly to the love and care of the couple. Most of them, however, didn't respond well when they first entered into the family. They didn't trust their new parents.

After months of consistent, patient affirmation and correction, after months of wiping up spills without condemning the children, after months of reading to them and playing with them, the message started to sink into these children's minds and hearts one by one. They could trust their new parents. They could have a new identity.

We are like these children. Some of us can respond to our adopted Father fairly easily. Some of us need a little more time to understand His love and care so we can trust Him, feel close to Him, and obey Him. How we think about God and about ourselves determines virtually every attitude and action in our lives. Until we are convinced that our new Father is loving and strong, we will continue to be bitter and self-reliant or fearful and withdrawn. We desperately need to comprehend our new identity as adopted children of God.

It is not a question of *whether* God loves us or not. It is a question of our *perception* of His love and power. Sometimes even people who are deeply loved and thoroughly cared for have a poor perception of God. Most of us can readily tell the story of the prodigal son in Luke 15. The younger son asked for his share of an inheritance and after receiving it, wasted it in an immoral lifestyle. When he found himself totally destitute, he realized that he could ask his father to let him be a lowly hired hand. But when he went to his home, his father lovingly forgave him and reinstated him to full privileges as his son. End of story? Not quite.

The older brother was in the field when he heard the sound of music and dancing. A celebration of some kind was going on. When a servant reported that the festivities were in honor of his wayward younger brother, who had selfishly wasted part of the family fortune, and that his father had forgiven him and tenderly received him back into the family, he was furious!

The father begged him to come join the party, but the older brother retorted:

> *... Look! For so many years I have been serving you, and I have never neglected a command of yours; and yet you have never given me a kid, that I might be merry with my friends; but when this son of yours came, who has devoured your wealth with harlots, you killed the fattened calf for him.* Luke 15:29-30

He had worked hard all his life and had never been given a party like his degenerate brother had received. He was bitter and jealous. The father responded gently:

> *...My child, you have always been with me, and all that is mine is yours. But we had to be merry and rejoice, for this brother of yours was dead and has begun to live, and was lost and has been found.*   Luke 15:31-32

The father was obviously kind and generous to both sons, but the older brother had never noticed. He had missed out on both the intimacy and the blessings that his father would have gladly given him. His younger brother, who had come back expecting to be a field hand, was experiencing the blessings of being a beloved son. In contrast, the older brother, who had been around his loving father all of his life, saw himself as only a field hand. His poor perception of his father had cost him dearly!

We use the term "child of God" quite often, but what does it mean? What difference does it make? How can a person experience the intimacy and blessing of being God's child? The Bible and doctrine of adoption gives us a clear perception of our relationship with God.

John Stott capsulized the New Testament teaching on adoption:

> *...it was Jesus himself who always addressed God intimately as "Abba, Father," who gave us permission to do the same, approaching Him as "our Father in heaven." The apostles enlarged on it. John, who attributes our being children of God to our being born of God, expresses his sense of wonder that the Father should have loved us enough to call us, and indeed make us, His children. Paul, on the other hand, traces our status as God's children rather to our adoption than to our new birth, and emphasizes the privilege we have in being sons instead of slaves, and therefore heirs as well."* [1]

The truth of our adoption teaches us that we have the security, intimacy, and the provision of God. God Himself initiated our adoption as His sons and daughters, therefore, we are secure (Gal. 4:4-6). We are the recipients of the spirit of adoption which overcomes and casts out the fearful spirit of slavery (Rom. 8:15). Our status as God's children is made possible entirely by His grace (Titus 3:3-7) so that our security is based on His strong love and power, not on our self-righteous efforts and fickle emotions.

Through our adoption, we have more than legal standing with God (wonderful as that is!). We have intimacy with Him. In the Old Testament, the mighty character of God produced a sense of fear and dread in men. The New Testament keeps this sense of the awesomeness of God, but it also adds the truth that this mighty God is the Father of believers. Instead of shrinking back in terror or dread, we are encouraged to *"draw near with confidence to the throne of grace, that we may receive mercy and may find grace to help in time of need."* (Heb. 4:16) Though God is the majestic, sovereign, omnipotent Creator, we can actually have an intimate relationship with Him. We are assured by the inner witness of the Spirit (Rom. 8:16) as He communicates both His love and His direction (Rom. 8:14). And Paul gives us the overwhelming reason why God wants us to experience this intimacy with Him. It is because of *"the kind intention of His will, to the praise of the glory of His grace, which He freely bestowed on us in the Beloved."* (Eph. 1:5-6) What a statement of the Lord's strong affection toward us!

When He adopted us as His children, the Lord pledged Himself to provide for us. Jesus assured us of the Father's generous response to our needs:

> *Ask , and it shall be given to you; seek, and you shall find; knock, and it shall be opened to you. For everyone who asks receives, and he who seeks finds, and to him who knocks it shall be opened. Or what man is there among you, when his son shall ask him for a loaf, will give him a stone? Or if he shall ask for a fish, he will not give him a snake, will he? If you then, being evil, know how to give good gifts to your children, how much more shall your Father who is in heaven give what is good to those who ask Him!*
>
> Matt. 7:7-11

He will provide for His children, but He has gone even further than that. He has given us, as His children, the status of being heirs of His promises, His purposes, and His provisions.

Our response to this kind of relationship is fairly predictable. When we begin to understand the fatherhood of God and our identity as His sons and daughters, we respond in affection by calling Him "Abba, Father" (Gal. 4:4-7 and Rom. 8:15). This is not an arms-length relationship; rather, it is one of depth, honesty, expression, and intimacy. We respond by taking steps to purify our motives and actions (II Cor. 6:14-7:1 and 1 John 3:3). We want to honor the One who is our Father. The intensity of our desire to honor Him enables us to suffer rejection and deprivation for His sake (Rom. 8:17). And we will love other members of the family of God, even if they are radically different from us (Eph. 2:11-22).

The more that we understand our identity as God's sons and daughters, the more we will sense the tremendous privilege it is to be a child of God. We will serve Him gladly and strive to honor Him at all costs. Instead of having a foot-dragging "have-to" attitude toward obeying and serving God, we will develop a "want-to" attitude.

But how does a person's sense of identity change? Some people have had parents who did a good job of modeling the character of God, so their identity of being a loved and accepted child of God is an easy transition from being a loved and accepted child in their families.

But how do people whose earthly parents neglected, abused, or manipulated them change their identity? These people need to contrast God the Father with their earthly parents, not equate Him with them. These people need to see differences between the Lord and their parents, not assume they are similar. They can say, *Even though my parents neglected me, the Lord never does. He cares for me and provides for me. Even though my parents didn't give me much attention, the Lord is always thinking about me. He knows every thought, feeling, and need I have.*

A person's identity changes as his perception of God and of himself changes. It usually takes a blend of three elements: cognitive, volitional, and relational. The consistent and specific study of God's word gives him the basic truths to meditate on. Then there are specific instances each day when choices can be made: *Will I respond like an unloved, cast-off orphan, or will I respond like a loved and accepted child of the Almighty God?* Third, he needs the modeling and affirmation of other members of God's family to help him understand and grow in his new identity.

When a ten-year-old child is adopted into a family, his new identity will grow and develop if these three elements are present. But there is one more crucial element: the active and specific help of the parent. If the child is struggling with his identity and asks the loving parents, "Will you please help me?" they will respond with compassion and strong action.

It is the same with our adopted Father. If we are struggling to understand and apply our new identity as His child, we can ask Him for help. The Holy Spirit is our helper, and He will give us the wisdom and courage we need to live in our new identities.

There are many ways to describe the characteristics of a child of God. God's initiative to give His children security, intimacy, and provisions yields an affectionate and deep response in us. Let's look at five characteristics of children of God:

1. God is their refuge.

Are you fearful? Does an unexplainable dread prevail in your thoughts, or do you experience a peace that goes beyond your normal responses to stress?

When we experience difficulties, we are quick to look for solutions. But usually those solutions consist of our own wisdom and our own strength, or the wisdom, strength, and resources of some other person or organization. Why do we look for solutions everywhere and anywhere else except the Lord when He is so wise, loving, and powerful? No matter how much ability we possess, no matter how much ability others possess, the Lord has far more! He may use our resources or the resources of others to meet our needs, but He is our refuge. He is the one who gives wisdom, strength, and peace. Three classic passages communicate this truth:

God is our refuge and strength, a very present help in trouble.
Therefore we will not fear, though the earth should change,
and though the mountains slip into the heart of the sea; though its
waters roar and foam, though the mountains quake at its swelling
pride. [Selah.]

Ps. 46:1-3

Trust in the LORD with all your heart, and do not lean on your
own understanding. In all your ways acknowledge Him, and He
will make your paths straight.   Prov. 3:5-6

Peace I leave with you; My peace I give to you: not as the world
gives, do I give to you. Let not your heart be troubled, nor let it be
fearful.

John 14:27

In any and all circumstances, remember, God is our refuge.

2. God is their source of supply.

Often in our daydreams, we wish we had someone who would supply us with all our needs. We do! Our Heavenly Father can–and will–supply them. It is because we do not understand His character and have developed alternate supply lines, that we think God really doesn't supply our needs.

Here's a painful test: think about all the things you own. Who supplied them? When we think of our possessions as being supplied without God's intervention, we reveal our true belief system.

One Christian honestly confessed: "When I think about my house and car, I believe they resulted from my job. Actually, when I look around my house, I think of each bit of furniture as being supplied by a source other than God. My parents gave me the living room furniture for a wedding present. My wife bought me my favorite chair. Many other items were bought on an installment plan, with the help of my bank. In all honesty, I don't really think much at all about God being my Provider."

It takes some serious thinking to recognize that we can and must look to our Father as our Provider. In fact, our jobs and possessions are really not ours. They were provided by Him and they belong to Him at all times.

3. They know they are precious to God.

Our Father is so concerned about us that He knows when we lose a hair from our heads (Matt. 10:30). He never ceases to love, to nurture, to care, and protect us. We are very special to Him!

The apostle Peter wrote to comfort and encourage the Christian Jews who had been scattered because of persecution:

> *And coming to Him as to a living stone, rejected by men, but choice and precious in the sight of God, you also, as living stones, are being built up as a spiritual house for a holy priesthood, to offer up spiritual sacrifices acceptable to God through Jesus Christ.*
>
> 1 Pet. 2:4-5

In this passage, Peter explains that Christ is a *"living stone"* rejected by men and that He is *"choice and precious in the sight of God."* Then Peter identifies us with Christ and says that we, too, are living stones, choice and precious in the sight of God.

But Peter doesn't stop there. He then describes the results of understanding this wonderful identity. Those who realize that they are precious to God learn to abhor sin the way God does. Their passion in life is to honor the Lord through love, obedience, and service.

Our status before God is one of great security and significance. Peter goes on to capsulize our position in Christ and our subsequent response in verse 9:

But you are "a chosen race," a royal "priesthood," "a holy nation, a people for God's own possession," that you may proclaim the excellencies of Him who has called you out of darkness into His marvelous light.

1 Pet. 2:9

We have great worth because of our relationship with God. As we are increasingly convinced of our new worth and identity, we will want to honor Him more and more.

4. God is worshipped.

Consider the emotions of a young man or woman who has fallen in love. He or she will experience tremendous joy and excitement when it is time for the loved one to arrive.

What about your emotions when it's time for your personal Bible study and devotions? Does worship bore you, or do you get excited when you prepare to meet with God?

If we really see Him as our Father, we will recognize that God is both loving and majestic. He delights to be worshipped! And He is worthy of our praise and obedience.

But worship is not based just on an emotion; it is an act of the will. No matter what our emotions are like (happy or sad, glad or angry, thankful or sullen), we choose to reflect on the character of God. Perhaps thinking about His faithfulness will encourage us when we are depressed, or perhaps as we think about His love, we will realize that we haven't been loving to someone in particular. If that's the case, we can confess our sin to God (and perhaps to that person, too!), and then rejoice in His grace and faithfulness more fully.

5. God reigns over them.

Our world has the mistaken opinion that man can dictate his terms to

God and tell Him how we will relate to Him. Rom. 1:21-25 tells us about the rebellious spirit of the human race:

> *For although they knew God, they neither glorified him as God nor gave thanks to him, but their thinking became futile and their foolish hearts were darkened. Although they claimed to be wise, they became fools and exchanged the glory of the immortal God for images made to look like mortal man and birds and animals and reptiles. Therefore God gave them over in the sinful desires of their hearts to sexual impurity for the degrading of their bodies with one another. They exchanged the truth of God for a lie, and worshipped and served created things rather than the Creator—who is forever praised. Amen.*

Many of us have fallen into the trap of trying to make God our servant instead of our ruler. Then, when God does not react in the way we want Him to, we become angry with Him. But God relates to us on the basis of who He truly is, and not as we think Him to be.

At the time of conversion, we are rescued from eternal condemnation, granted status as children of God, and given a sense of purpose. At that point, we are to surrender our lives to Him. We are not to withhold any area of our life from His right to reign over it.

Later, the Holy Spirit will reveal areas in our lives which are not under the total Lordship of Christ. We are to then yield those areas as He makes us aware of them.

It is imperative that we have a clear understanding of the nature and the character of Christ. As our Savior, He rescues us from a selfish and ultimately empty lifestyle. As our Lord, He is our acknowledged owner and master. We are His bondservants, delighting to do the will of the One who loved us enough to rescue us from hell and give us peace and purpose.

His word is our final authority. The Bible is the inspired guidebook for us, and if we believe the Bible is God's message to us, we will not use it as just an ornament to carry in and out of church services. Reading it will have a daily, vital priority in our lives because we will see our need to draw on its insight, wisdom, strength, and comfort.

If the Lord is to rule over us on a moment by moment basis, we must look toward Him and let His word speak to us. Memorizing verses, "hiding them in our hearts," is an excellent way to remember His Lordship over us. In reading the Gospels, note how many times the writers quote Scriptures from the Old Testament. Before they could do that, they had to know the Scriptures intimately.

Knowing God's word was no more important for them than it is for us. We cannot accurately interpret life around us unless we do so in light of the Scriptures. And we cannot know the Scriptures unless we are prepared to spend time studying them.

In addition, we are the Lord's bondslaves. Being a bondslave is a deliberate choice. The term comes from Ex. 21:5-6:

> *But if the servant declares, "I love my master and my wife and children and do not want to go free," then his master must take him before the judges* [or before God]. *He shall take him to the door or the doorpost and pierce his ear with an awl. Then he will be his servant for life.*

The voluntary commitment of the servant to his master is a deliberate one with far-reaching consequences. Paul often referred to himself as a bondslave of Jesus Christ. The deliberate surrender of his life was total.

God is our loving and powerful Father. He is worthy of our affection, our obedience, and our service.

[1]John R.W. Stott, *The Cross Of Christ* (Downers Grove, IL: IVP, 1986), pp. 193-194.

Seven

THE NAMES OF GOD

It is vitally important that we create an accurate category for the Lord based upon the truth of Scripture. As we do, we will form a new foundation for our lives; a new source of love, faith, and obedience. By changing our understanding of who He is, we will draw closer to Him.

What's in a Name?

There are many descriptive names for God in the Bible. Most of them are translated as "God," or "Lord," or "Lord God," but they are actually much more descriptive and meaningful than that. God's names are important because every one of them reveals something special about His character. They are not names attached to Him by man. His names are His own selection, used to reveal Himself in all His fullness. So sacred are the names presented in this chapter that one-third of the Ten Commandments forbids their use in any flippant manner. Aspects of His nature revealed through His names should not be regarded frivolously.

Many years ago, names did more than identify people. They were associated with the personality and characteristics of a person. In ancient times, a person's name was much more than a way to identify family relationships. They were used to designate a particular characteristic of the person named. An example of this is found in the name of Jacob, meaning "Supplanter." He was a crafty, self-seeking person until he met God. After his encounter with the angel of the Lord, his name was changed to Israel, meaning "He struggles with God."

In the third chapter of Exodus, God commissioned Moses to free Israel from Egyptian bondage. In verses 13 and 14, Moses said to God,

> *"Suppose I go to the Israelites and say to them, 'The God of your fathers has sent me to you,' and they ask me, 'What is his name?' Then what shall I tell them?"* God said to Moses, *"I AM WHO I AM.* [JEHOVAH] *This is what you are to say to the Israelites: 'I AM has sent me to you.'"*

JEHOVAH is a very significant name for God because it states that He is eternal and self-existent.

This name gave a new credibility to Moses, the man who was identified with it. Throughout the difficulties of his confrontations with Pharaoh, the Exodus, and the forty years in the wilderness, Moses knew he could trust Jehovah.

By examining some of God's other names, we can learn more about His character.

Three Primary Names for God

ELOHIM (God)

This Hebrew word is a combination of two words: EL, meaning "unlimited strength, energy, might, and power" and ALAH, meaning "to swear, declare, or make a covenant." Together, they describe God as One of infinite strength and faithfulness.

The first mention of God in Gen. 1:1 refers to Him as ELOHIM: *In the beginning God created the heavens and the earth.* Jesus used this term in Matt. 19:26 when He said, *"With man this is impossible, but with God* (ELOHIM) *all things are possible."* In this case, His endless power is revealed by the use of the name.

ELOHIM is a plural word. Although God is a single deity, His trinitarian nature is clearly stated by the plural use of the word. For example, Deut. 4:35 emphasizes the *unity* of the Godhead:

You were shown these things so that you might know that the Lord is God [ELOHIM]*; besides him there is no other.*

Genesis 1:26, on the other hand, emphasizes the *plurality* within the Godhead: *"Let us make man in our image, in our likeness..."* This passage is our first introduction to the Trinity: the Father, Son, and Holy Spirit.

In Heb. 1:3 we are told:

The Son is the radiance of God's [ELOHIM'S] *glory and the exact representation of his being, sustaining all things by his powerful word.*

Jesus Christ has revealed the One to us who always keeps His covenant with man. He will do what He has sworn to do. His power is constant. It doesn't waver.

James 1:17 says:

Every good and perfect gift is from above, coming down from the Father of the heavenly lights, who does not change like shifting shadows.

When we know and depend on His covenant promises, we may be sure He will not change His mind. He has sufficient power to create all things and to sustain them. He never makes a promise to do something and then becomes too busy to keep it. He is totally dependable. Perhaps your father often promised to do things for you or with you, and then didn't follow through. If your "father category" has been shaped by an undependable parent, and if you now find it difficult to trust God, then this name for God will be important to you. By His very nature, He cannot break His covenant promises with us!

ELOHIM is a name for God which will enrich your prayer life. It will continually remind you of His limitless power, and that He always, *always* keeps His promises. Think about this name when you are claiming His promises to you as recorded in His word.

JEHOVAH (Lord God)

Meaning "HE WHO IS TRULY PRESENT," this name describes God as the dependable and faithful God who can be fully trusted. It can also mean, "I will always be what I have always been."

Jehovah is the personal name for God. While ELOHIM speaks of His power, JEHOVAH speaks of His intimate relationship with us. God took the initiative with Moses and the Israelites, stepping deliberately into the lives of people who were slaves.

When you feel that God isn't really interested in you and your problems, remember the meaning of God's name, JEHOVAH! This name is connected with His mighty acts of setting people free, of redeeming them from bondage. It assures you that God is personally and vitally interested in every single thing about you, and that He is committed to leading you to a solution for your difficulties. As a Father who cares, He will not be bored by the sharing of your difficulties with Him.

Jesus referred to Himself in John 8:58 by saying,

I tell you the truth, before Abraham was born, I am!

He did not say "I was," but "I *Am*," using the word JEHOVAH. Once again, we are reminded that Christ has fully revealed the Father to us.

In studying passages where JEHOVAH is used, we learn that God existed before anything had been created, that He is holy, that He hates and judges sin, and that He loves and saves sinners. In all cases where it is used, His deeply personal relationship with us is the focus of the name.

In reading the first five books of the Bible, it is fascinating to note how the writer sometimes refers to God as ELOHIM and at other times as JEHOVAH. In each case, a different emphasis is being made about His character. The Powerful One is also the Personal One, who numbers every hair on our heads and who sees every tiny sparrow that falls to the ground. In fact, an entire series of descriptive words are attached to this name so that we can understand more about God's character. We will review these later in this chapter.

ADONAI (Lord)

In Josh. 3:11, God is called *"Lord* [ADONAI] *of all the earth."* As with ELOHIM, this word for God is in the plural, again pointing to the Trinity. It refers to God's role as one high and above all things, the Owner of all there is.

The name ADONAI is often coupled with JEHOVAH to remind us that although we have an intimate relationship with God, He is, nevertheless, not to be viewed as a human counterpart.

This word for God emphasizes that He is Lord and Master, "one who exercises rule and authority." The emphasis is on a relationship between a master and a servant. Our Master has the right to expect absolute obedience from us. In return, we have the right to expect provision and direction from our benevolent Master.

Being a servant to ADONAI is a fantastic arrangement! We have the privilege of representing the God of the universe. What could bring greater meaning to our activities? In return, He provides all the resources needed to do His will. We become His resource to perform His activity on the earth, and our resources are freely given to us by Him.

When you see yourself as a servant of ADONAI, you will be thankful that He will provide for all of your needs. You will also recognize the necessity for being obedient to His guidance because He knows best and He has your welfare in mind.

Scholars have discovered the word ADONAI was not used by any other ancient civilization–only Israel! It's a special word, used to reveal a special relationship between God and those who are closely related to Him.

Do you sometimes use the English term "Master" or "Lord" in your prayers? As you use them, remember the One who exercises rule and authority, and then respond in faith, obedience, and glad service to Him.

The Nine Compound Names for God

In addition to the three primary names for God, there are several combinations of names which describe His character:

EL SHADDAI (God Almighty)

The Scripture emphasizes the Lord's nature as the giver and sustainer of life in the name EL SHADDAI. SHADDAI is taken from the Hebrew word SHAD, meaning "breast." Even as a mother breast-feeds her child, so God is described as One who feeds and nurtures His own. The term is used in Gen. 17:1, Gen. 28:1-4, and Ps. 91:1.

The name is used in intimate and personal circumstances in the Old Testament. For example, God is called by this name in reference to the birth of Isaac–the miracle child born to a man and woman too old to expect a baby.

EL SHADDAI was the One who made provisions for poor Hagar and her son, Ishmael, when Sarah demanded that Abraham evict them from their household. He is the One who, today, will care for the fatherless and the homeless.

The name was used again when circumcision was instituted as a covenant sign between God and Israel. This rite, performed on every Israelite male, was a symbol of the special covenant relationship between God and His people.

You will want to use this name when you need God's care and provision.

EL ELYON (Most High God)

When this term is used, we are reminded that the Father is the possessor of heaven and earth. He is the omnipotent, Almighty God. This description is found in Gen. 14:18-23, Ps. 83:18, and Dan. 5:18.

This name demonstrates God's supremacy over all pagan deities. It literally means "the strongest strong one."

This does not suggest that there are any other gods in the universe who are less powerful than EL ELYON. The pagan notion that He is the highest among a huge community of gods is absurd, because there is only one God. All the others are myths or demons. Nevertheless, there are still tens of thousands of so-called "gods" worshipped by Orientals, Asians,

Africans, and Indians. The power usually attributed to them is, in reality, the activity of Satan, who attempts to counterfeit the acts of God.

In Abidjan, the capital of the Ivory Coast in West Africa, the Christians fervently sing "Jesus is higher! Satan is lower! Jesus is higher! Satan is erased!" There will be conditions in each of our lives when we, like the Christians in Abidjan, can trust and triumphantly announce that our God is Most High...EL ELYON. As we encounter resistance while following God's will, either within or outside ourselves, we need to call upon EL ELYON.

EL OLAM (The Everlasting God)

The word OLAM means "eternal duration, everlasting, evermore; something secret, hidden, or concealed." When this name is used, our attention is directed to God's timelessness, His vast knowledge, and His constancy. The term is used, among other places, in Gen. 21:33, Ps. 90:1-2, and Deut. 33:27.

In Gen. 21:22-31, the patriarch, Abraham, had a confrontation with King Abimelech and Phicol, commander of the Philistine forces. When a treaty between them had been completed, Abraham planted a tree as a monument and called upon the name of EL OLAM (Gen. 21:33). He knew that these two men were as changeable as the weather, and that the treaty would be worthless apart from God's unchanging nature. In the next verse, we are told, *"And Abraham stayed in the land of the Philistines for a long time."* EL OLAM was his security!

Moses is the author of Psalm 90. In it, he meditates on the eternal presence of God. He refers to EL OLAM when, in verses 1 and 2, he says,

> *Lord, you have been our dwelling place throughout all genera-*
> *ions. Before the mountains were born or you brought forth the*
> *earth and the world, from everlasting to everlasting you are*
> *God* [EL OLAM].

These verses transcend time and space, causing us to recall that our Heavenly Father is unlimited by conditions which restrict and inhibit us.

In Deut. 33:27, Moses again uses this word for God in his final address to his people:

> *The eternal God* [EL OLAM] *is your refuge, and underneath are the everlasting arms.*

How comforting it must have been to Moses to entrust his beloved Israel to such a God!

The nature of God, as revealed in the name EL OLAM, will be very important to you when you must trust God and God alone with situations where His stability is all you have to depend on. That was precisely the situation a couple found themselves in, when their teenage son ran away from home. For several days, they suffered the agony of not knowing if he was alive or dead, or whether they would ever see him again. As they prayed, they called upon EL OLAM, and He gave them His peace which surpasses understanding.

He will do the same for you. When conditions get stormy, speak His name with peace in your heart.

EL ROI (The God Who Sees)

The Hebrew name ROI means "the one who sees." Our God is revealed to be One who watches over us, concerning Himself with our needs. He sees that our needs are met. He also sees our every thought, word, and deed. Passages using this term include Gen. 16:13-14 and Heb. 4:13.

Hagar's condition was miserable. First, her mistress, Sarah, called upon her to become pregnant by her husband. Then, in a fit of jealousy, Sarah threw her out of the house while she was carrying the unborn child. Without a destination, Hagar found herself alone by a spring in the desert. Her loneliness and feelings of rejection were intense. In Gen. 16:7-12, God appeared to her, advising her to return to Sarah. He then told her he would increase her descendants through Ishmael. In verse 13 we read,

*She gave this name to the LORD who spoke to her: "You are the
God [EL ROI] who sees me," for she said, "I have now seen the
One who sees me."*

Does God know your condition? Of course! He is EL ROI. Here
again we see the constant theme in these names for God: His awareness of
everything about us.

If your earthly father failed to mirror this understanding and
awareness of your needs, you will want to reflect on the truth that God is
with you constantly, understanding all your circumstances and able to
meet all your needs.

These marvelous names are only the beginning of His revelation
about Himself. We shall now consider eight compound names related to
the name JEHOVAH.

JEHOVAH-JIREH (The Lord Will Provide)

The name JIREH means "to see to it or to provide." The use of the
term involves references to His testing of us after he has prepared us to
meet and pass the test.

This concept appears in Gen. 22:8 and again in Phil. 4:19 where He
promises to *"meet all your needs according to His glorious riches in
Christ Jesus."*

In Gen. 22:1-19, Abraham's relationship with God and with his son,
Isaac, is severely tested. He faces the important question of which one is
most precious to him. Obeying God completely, he plans to sacrifice his
child as requested. As they climb together to the altar site, Isaac asks,
"Where is the lamb for the burnt offering?" Abraham responds, *"God
Himself* [JEHOVAH-JIREH] *will provide the lamb..."*

It's hard to imagine a better way to illustrate the significance of this
word than through this story. God never intended for Abraham to kill
Isaac. He wanted Abraham to demonstrate that his love for God was
greater than his love for his son. Abraham prepared to follow through
with God's demand, but the Lord stopped him. His provision was a ram, a

substitute sacrifice for Isaac. We must always remember that JEHOVAH-JIREH presented a substitute for us, too. The Lamb of God was Jesus Christ. He came "to provide for" our sin problem by providing us with the only possible solution to our separation from God.

If He cared enough to go to the cross to provide our most fundamental spiritual need, then we may be certain that He will not stop there. He provided a dry path through the Red Sea for Israel. He provided release from a prison cell for Peter. He still provides all we need to walk with Him. Paul states in Rom. 8:32:

> *He who did not spare His own Son, but delivered Him up for us all, how will He not also with Him freely give us all things?*

The Lord is gracious and generous, but don't use this name to manipulate Him to get your selfish wants! Those who have tried to manipulate God have been disillusioned by His lack of cooperation. As a perfect Father, He knows *what* we need, and He knows *when* we need it. Understanding *His* will and *His* purpose will save us a lot of frustration in expecting His provisions to be what *we* want, when *we* want them.

JEHOVAH-NISSI (The Lord My Banner)

The word NISSI refers to a banner, an emblem, a war flag. This description of the character of God refers to men going into conflict. Flying as a banner before them is JEHOVAH-NISSI. This wonderful name reminds us that all power is with Him and all strength for battle comes from Him. He will lead us to victory. In Ex. 17:15, after Moses won a victory over Amalek he built a memorial altar and called it "The Lord is My Banner."

Another place where the term is found is in Isaiah 59. Isaiah sees the corruption in Israel. In verse 14, he says,

> *...justice is driven back...truth has stumbled in the streets, honesty cannot enter.*

When God saw this lack of justice, He was *"appalled that there was no one to intervene."* Who would care for the helpless ones who were prey for the greedy? The answer is given in verse 19:

> *From the west, men will fear the name of the Lord, and from the rising of the sun, they will revere his glory. For he will come like a pent-up flood that the breath of the Lord* [JEHOVAH-NISSI] *drives along.*

They were not alone in their struggle. JEHOVAH flew over them like a victory banner, like a mighty tidal wave of judgment blown along by the wind of His Spirit.

Sometimes we, too, find ourselves seemingly helpless before circumstances. In those cases, we can raise our Banner high, and we can remember that JEHOVAH-NISSI is our strength and our shield in our battles.

JEHOVAH-TSIDKENU (The Lord Our Righteousness)

TSIDKENU, added to JEHOVAH, reminds us that God is the only truly righteous One. He Himself is the absolute, impeccable standard. We are reminded that perfect righteousness is the natural attribute of God, and that it cannot be found elsewhere. This name is a reminder that the only righteousness we will ever have is His righteousness.

In Ex. 9:27, the term is used by Pharaoh. Plague upon plague had caused him to see the mighty power of God until he was brought to understand the contrast between himself and Israel's deity:

> *Then Pharaoh summoned Moses and Aaron. "This time I have sinned," he said to them. "The Lord* [JEHOVAH-TSIDKENU] *is in the right, and I and my people are in the wrong."*

In Jeremiah 23, the Lord is disgusted with those who were supposed to care for Israel. In verse 1, they are described as unrighteous *"shepherds who are destroying and scattering the sheep."* It is then that the prophecy is given in verses 5 and 6:

> *"The days are coming," declares the Lord, "when I will raise up to David* [or up from David's line] *a righteous Branch, a King who will reign wisely and do what is just and right in the land. In his days Judah will be saved and Israel will live in safety. This is the name by which he will be called: The Lord Our Righteousness* [JEHOVAH-TSIDKENU]*."*

Our right standing before God is not based on how good we are. (If it were, we would be in big trouble!) It is based on the greatest swap in history: the Lord took our sins and we received His righteousness. Paul describes this exchange in his second letter to the believers in Corinth:

> *For God took the sinless Christ and poured into him our sins. Then, in exchange, he poured God's goodness into us!*
>
> II Cor. 5:21, *The Living Bible*

We can take comfort from Paul's comment in II Tim. 4:8:

> *Now there is in store for me the crown of righteousness, which the Lord, the righteous Judge, will award to me on that day—and not only to me, but also to all who have longed for his appearing.*

The Lord is a righteous judge and He will give eternal rewards to those who love, honor, and obey Him.

JEHOVAH-RAAH (The Lord My Shepherd)

God, as our Shepherd, is revealed in this compound name. He is seen as One tending, pasturing, leading, feeding, and protecting. As His sheep, we are completely dependent upon our Good Shepherd. His compassion for us is so complete that He laid down His life for His sheep, and He will gather us as a flock when He returns to the earth. Examples of this concept are found in Ps. 23, Num. 27:16-17, Ezek. 34:23, Matt. 9:36, and Rev. 7:16-17.

One of the interesting things about this name for God is that it communicates our status as sheep. Of all God's creatures, none has a poorer sense of direction. They are also one of the few animals who have no means of protecting themselves. When wolves attack them, they simply panic, running around until they're killed. They must be constantly watched, protected, and found when they've strayed off.

Reflect on this name for God the next time you face a decision and don't know what choice to make. Think about it when you are under attack and can't defend yourself. Remember it when you feel that your life has just fallen off a cliff, and you are clinging, helpless and frightened, to the last limb you can reach. He is JEHOVAH-RAAH at such times for you.

JEHOVAH-RAPHA (The Lord That Heals)

The Hebrew word RAPHA means "to cure, to heal, to restore." Our Lord is described as the One who will heal the physical, the moral, and the spiritual illnesses of His children. While in His sovereignty He does not always choose to heal our physical ailments, He has the power to do so. This lovely name is found in Ex. 15:26:

> *He said, "If you listen carefully to the voice of the Lord your God and do what is right in his eyes, if you pay attention to his commands and keep all his decrees, I will not bring on you any of the diseases I brought on the Egyptians, for I am the Lord [JEHOVAH-RAPHA], who heals you."*

In Matt. 9:12, Jesus spoke of spiritual healing as He said, *"It is not the healthy who need a doctor, but the sick."* Peter reminds us that JEHOVAH-RAPHA *"bore our sins in his body on the tree...by his wounds you have been healed."* (I Pet. 2:24)

Today, a ministry called RAPHA cares for those suffering from emotional distresses and/or substance abuse. This organization takes literally the promise that God is our healer, and it applies sound, biblical principles to bring JEHOVAH-RAPHA to hurting lives.

Call upon God by this name when you need healing. Shattered marriages can be healed, and so can those ugly memories of past events. Children who have become rebellious can be restored. Physical illnesses can be touched and destructive habits changed by His power.

JEHOVAH-SHALOM (The Lord My Peace)

Most of us are familiar with the Hebrew word, SHALOM, meaning "peace." This term describes the end of all strife and conflict, the removal of everything that causes division or destroys harmony. Other words used to describe its meaning include wholeness, completeness, being well or perfect, harmony of relationships with God, and reconciliation based on a completed transaction. You will find this concept used as the basis for Eph. 2:14-17 and Col. 1:20.

Don't miss the important fact that peace is not found in a condition, but in a Person. We may try to find peace by security alarm systems, vacations in the mountains, or soothing music, but Jesus said He would bring a special kind of peace that the world couldn't give or take away. He is our peace.

Although Sharon worked in a church office, her work left her emotionally drained. There always seemed to be too many phone calls, too many deadlines, too many interruptions. She developed severe tension headaches.

Sensing her unrest, the church pastor began to be concerned about her. He asked her, "Sharon, is your life controlled by circumstances, or is it controlled by your relationship with the Lord?" At first, she resented the question. But as they began to talk about her past, she began to realize that her relationship with her father was a great part of her difficulty.

He was a drifter who frequently moved his family from town to town. By the time she entered the tenth grade, she had attended eleven schools. She married when she was seventeen to get away from home.

Sharon was finally able to say, "I have been controlled by all the circumstances of my life for as long as I can remember. For me, the Heavenly Father has never been a person I could trust."

Like others, she had used her "father category," based upon her experiences, to define God's character. As JEHOVAH-SHALOM slowly became more real to her, a new lifestyle developed. Even in the middle of phone calls, deadlines, and interruptions, Sharon began to experience God's peace, and she began to influence all who related to her. Sharon's years of being controlled by circumstances had begun to be replaced by a new perspective and attitude. Her tranquillity was in her newfound relationship with the Heavenly Father.

JEHOVAH-SABBAOTH (The Lord of Hosts)

SABBAOTH means "to mass together, to assemble for warfare." This is God's fighting name as the Lord of Hosts. He is the leader, the all-conquering Savior, the guide and guardian of His people. He is the commander of invisible armies.

Jerusalem had been reduced to a pile of rubble, and the temple was totally demolished. Judah lived as prisoners in Babylonia for many years. When Zechariah and Zerubbabel returned to Jerusalem, God told them to rebuild the temple.

It was an overwhelming request! It had taken all the wealth and influence of David and Solomon to build it the first time. *They* had all the resources of a healthy nation and almost unlimited manpower. Sister kingdoms had donated cedar and other building materials. How could these powerless men do so great a task?

In Zech. 4:6-10 the answer is given:

> *So he said to me, "This is the word of the LORD to Zerubbabel:*
> *'Not by might nor by power, but by my Spirit,' says the LORD*
> *Almighty* [JEHOVAH-SABBAOTH]. *What are you, O mighty*
> *mountain? Before Zerubbabel you will become level ground. Then*
> *he will bring out the capstone to shouts of 'God bless it! God bless*
> *it!'" Then the word of the LORD came to me: "The hands of*

> *Zerubbabel have laid the foundation of this temple; his hands will also complete it. Then you will know that the LORD Almighty [JEHOVAH-SABBAOTH] has sent me to you. Who despises the day of small things? Men will rejoice when they see the plumb line in the hand of Zerubbabel...."*

What battle do you face? Is He the commander-in-chief of your conflict? If so, you cannot lose even though the struggle may be long and the battle fierce! With JEHOVAH-SABBAOTH all things are possible.

JEHOVAH-SHAMMAH (The Lord Is Present)

SHAMMAH means "is present." With this beautiful term, God pledges His presence to us. Further, the name reminds us we cannot escape His presence. The term is found in Ezek. 48:35, Ps. 68:16, Gen. 31:3 and, in the New Testament, this idea is communicated in Matt. 28:19-20.

Corrie Ten Boom, author of *The Hiding Place*, had a habit some people found irritating. As she visited with someone, her lips often shaped words which could not be heard. On one occasion, a person talking to her stopped in the middle of a sentence and said, "Miss Ten Boom, are you saying something to me? I didn't catch it." She replied, "You must excuse an old woman. I was just talking to our Lord about what we are saying to each other." For her, JEHOVAH-SHAMMAH was a participant in her every conversation. His presence was her joy, His companionship as real as the presence of the people around her.

You, too, can delight in His constant presence. One man decided to turn off the radio in his car and use his commute each morning to communicate with the Lord. A mother chose to arise each morning one hour before the family to enjoy her morning coffee with JEHOVAH-SHAMMAH.

Generations ago, Brother Lawrence wrote a book on this subject that is still in print, a classic of Christian literature called *Practicing the Presence of God*. Perhaps it's time for you to discover what thousands of others have known: the Lord is never absent from you.

In a very real sense, the name JEHOVAH-SHAMMAH is a summary of all the other names of God. Whether your condition requires Him to provide, protect, defend, comfort, or guide, He is present with you and He will be what you need.

Meditate on these names of God. You will profit greatly by committing them to memory. For a few days, deliberately use them in the place of "Father" or "Lord" when you pray. Find peace, strength, and wisdom in your new knowledge of His character.

SECTION III

THE PROCESS: Changing Your Perception of God to
Experience His Love, Forgiveness, and Power

Eight

METAMORPHOSIS

Sam grew up in a home where his performance was highly scrutinized, but he was rarely affirmed. He was always encouraged to do better. His father was too busy in his business to spend time with him. His mother was a perfectionist, and nothing he did was ever quite good enough for her. Sam wanted more than anything to please his parents so that he could win their love. But his parents used this eagerness to manipulate him to do whatever they wanted him to, seldom giving him the reward of their praise and approval.

When I met Sam, he was a highly successful young man, but he was driven–driven to perform to earn the approval of others. No matter how well he did, he continued to feel a nagging sense of condemnation. We talked casually a few times, and I learned more about his family. Then one day he called me to ask how to cope with his parents.

As we talked, he realized that he had been manipulated by his parents all his life. They had withheld their love and affirmation so that he would feel compelled to do whatever they wanted him to. The need for approval is a compelling need! But this realization was a new revelation to Sam. He had never realized that the way he had been treated by his parents wasn't God's design for families. His family was obviously the only one he had ever been in, and he had nothing to compare it to. In his distorted perspective, he thought manipulation was normal.

Sam's view of God was based on his relationship with his parents. He saw God as aloof and demanding. He felt that he had to do everything "just right" for God. He tried to win approval by performing for the Lord just as he had for his parents, but the results were the same. He felt that he could never do enough for the Lord. He had a nagging sense of condemnation from the Lord based on his erroneous perceptions of Him.

How could Sam's view of God change? How could Sam experience the freshness and power of a strong, intimate relationship with God? Years of parental modeling had strongly influenced his view of God. What would change it?

There are four principles that define and describe the stages of our metamorphosis to a new perspective of God. These stages enable us to understand the process of change so that we will have hope for progress without being discouraged when "quick fixes" don't provide the help we need. These four stages are:

1. Recognizing the contrast between the character of God and that of your parents
2. Dwelling on the character of God as the source of security and significance
3. Choosing His love, forgiveness, and power at any and every given moment
4. Being patient; developing a "siege" mentality

Let's examine each of these.

1. Recognize the contrast between God's character and that of your parents.

This is an important first step. Until we correctly diagnose the problem, we cannot accurately apply God's solution. Some of us come from very stable, loving families, but many of us are like Sam. Because we have nothing to compare them with, we fail to see that our families aren't the kind that God has in mind.

No parents are perfect, and none of them perfectly communicates the loving and powerful character of God. But some do quite well. Some parents provide very good models for their children. They give unconditional love. They protect and provide for their children. And they give loving discipline to correct poor behavior.

Some parents, on the other hand, are guilty of neglect, abuse, and manipulation. They effectively destroy their children, who, apart from the grace and power of God, will reproduce the same pattern for generations to come.

The vast majority of parents fall between these extremes. We may think that Christian parents are always good models while unbelievers are always poor models, but that isn't the case. Even unbelieving parents can model the love, protection, and provision of God while, in some cases, Christian parents don't.

Both Christian and non-Christian parents may model some aspects of God's character well at one point in their lives, and poorly at other times. It's a mixed bag of signals, but remember, they're probably doing the best they know how to do based on the imperfect modeling they received!

When we begin to recognize the contrast between God's character and that of our parents, we may respond in a variety of ways. If the contrast isn't too great, we may instantly understand more of the love of God and rejoice in our newer and deeper understanding of His love and power. But if the contrast *is* great, we may experience an initial stage of anger and resentment. That's not wrong! It is a part of the healing process, and it should not be repressed. (For a better understanding of how to handle your emotions, see Chapter Eleven.)

2. Dwell on God's character: the source of your security and significance.

After you recognize the contrast between your parents' character and the character of God, spend a lot of time studying the love, forgiveness and power of God. He is the source of our security and significance. He is the One who loves us perfectly. The famous French philosopher and physicist, Blaise Paschal, said of Christ's exclusive ability to meet our needs:

> *There is a God-shaped vacuum in the heart of each man which cannot be filled by any created thing, but by God the Creator, made known through Jesus Christ.*

Even if no one else loves you, Christ loves you deeply. Even if no one else accepts you, the Lord accepts you unconditionally. Even if no one else will forgive you, Christ's death is the payment and the proof of His complete forgiveness. We need to dwell on these powerful and transforming truths day after day.

"A chapter a day keeps the devil away" may be a cute saying for vacation Bible school, but it takes concerted effort, study, and focused prayer to transform our minds and change our perspective of God. The modeling of a lifetime doesn't change easily. We would do well to plan regular times to study, to think, to pray, and to memorize the truths of God's Word so that His truth fills our minds and changes our hearts.

3. Choose His love, forgiveness, and power at any and every given moment.

The process of changing our perceptions of God involves a few monumental decisions; decisions to see the difference between our parents and God; decisions to feel the pain and enter the process of healing; decisions to take time to study God's word and to pray.

But the metamorphosis of these perceptions also involves a multitude of daily decisions to choose the love, forgiveness and power of God as our source of security and significance. The shift from getting our sense of self-worth from our parents to getting it from the Lord is a difficult one, but it is necessary. The Lord is loving and faithful. We can trust Him completely. David wrote about this transition:

> *For my father and my mother have forsaken me, but the Lord will take me up.*
>
> Ps. 27:10

Isaiah also wrote that the Lord's love far surpasses even that of a mother's:

Can a woman forget her nursing child, and have no compassion on the son of her womb? Even these may forget, but I will not forget you.

Is. 49:15

When a farmer's well runs dry, he digs a new one to meet the needs of his family and farm. When an army runs out of supplies, they do whatever it takes to provide for the needs of the soldiers. When we realize that no human being can meet our needs for security and significance, we must go to the source of abundant affirmation and purpose: Jesus Christ. We can (we must!) cling to Him. He is worthy of our affection and obedience.

A commitment to radical thankfulness is helpful in enabling us to make these daily choices. When someone's disapproval threatens to crush you, when you fail in an important task, when you don't feel like you look your best, when you are feeling introspective and depressed, or when you are angry...be honest about how you feel and choose to give thanks for God's love, purpose, and power.

Notice that we didn't say to *feel* thankful. You can't control your feelings but you can choose—as an act of your will—to dwell on the character of God, thanking Him for His compassion for you and His direction for your life, knowing that He can use any situation for good.

Radical thankfulness rivets our attention on the Lord, not on the fickle approval of others or the often distressing circumstances of life. It is often helpful to have the encouragement of a support group as you learn to make these choices, and fairly easy to find others who want to have their perceptions of God changed. Most people learn best when there is a combination of both cognitive teaching and relational reinforcement. You may want to find one friend or a small group to go through this book and workbook with you. It can be a rich time of interaction, and can facilitate the process of change a great deal.

4. Be patient; develop a "siege" mentality.

Quick fixes sound great, but they seldom work. For most of us, deep issues take time. Don't look for an instant solution to the transformation of your perception of God. It took time to develop a poor one; it will take time to change it. It is a process.

Most people experience both the flash of insight and the grind of change. They have a sudden realization of the problem or solution, but the application of that realization is often painfully slow. If they expect it to be rapid and for healing to occur overnight, they will be quickly discouraged. They may even quit the process altogether.

When a Roman army attacked a fortified city, the commander didn't shoot a couple of arrows and expect the city to fall. The army spent months and sometimes years in siege warfare. It was slow and tedious, but it was usually successful.

Our warfare against our inaccurate perceptions of God is like siege warfare. It is slow and tedious, but if we stay with it, there's great hope for success. Paul wrote of this warfare to the believers in Corinth:

> *For though we walk in the flesh, we do not war according to the flesh, for the weapons of our warfare are not of the flesh, but divinely powerful for the destruction of fortresses. We are destroying speculations and every lofty thing raised up against the knowledge of God, and we are taking every thought captive to the obedience of Christ....*
>
> II Cor. 10:3-5

The misconceptions we have about God are *speculations*. Our wrong perceptions are *"lofty things raised up against the knowledge of God."* These are fortresses that require a siege mentality, patience, and endurance. In the end, the walls will fall and the captives will be released.

You may gain a flash of insight and experience a surge of change at the beginning of your metamorphosis, but don't be discouraged if you don't experience complete emotional healing and transformation overnight. Realize that it takes time to change our fundamental perceptions about God and about ourselves. Realize that the Word of God and the power of His Spirit are a powerful combination. The process may be slow and it may be painful, but it's worth it.

As you go through these stages, remember to be kind to your parents. No, they weren't perfect, and they may have harmed you terribly. But they were probably doing the best they knew how to do. Even if they weren't, you can extend the love and forgiveness of God to them as you learn to experience it yourself.

This chapter has explained the process of change. The next one identifies what is needed for change to occur.

The workbook section of this book is designed to facilitate your study and application of God's truth. This chapter will become more significant to you as you spend time on the exercises and studies in the workbook.

Nine

"AND YOU SHALL KNOW THE TRUTH..."

As you have read the previous chapters of this book, you have probably recognized that your perception of God has been significantly shaped by the modeling of your parents. For some people, this evokes pleasant memories of a loving and protective family, but for others these memories are painful. For all of us, the question is, *How can our perception of God become a more exact representation of who He truly is?*

First, you must examine your present relationship with God. Many people think they are automatically born as children of God. That is not what the Bible teaches. In John 8:44, Jesus said to the Pharisees, *"You belong to your father, the devil, and you want to carry out your father's desire."* Since Satan is the father of lies, it's not hard to understand why we have believed so many untrue things about God.

How long ago did you receive Christ as your Savior and trust Him to make you a child of God? John tells us that to all who have received Jesus as Lord and Savior, He *"...gave the right to become children of God—children born not of natural descent, nor of human decision or a husband's will, but born of God."* (John 1:12-13)

This new life as a child of God is not the result of our good works or our penance. It is a gift, paid for at the cross by Jesus. Through the Father's grace, we are adopted as joint heirs with Christ, with all the rights and privileges of sonship immediately granted.

The Lord has reserved many blessings for us which we can increasingly experience as our distorted perceptions of Him are changed into accurate perceptions. Paul tells us in Rom. 12:2,

Do not conform any longer to the pattern of this world, but be transformed by the renewing of your mind. Then you will be able to test and approve what God's will is–his good, pleasing and perfect will.

To change our relationship with God, we must replace our wrong perceptions with reality. The way we think affects the way we feel. The way we feel often determines the way we act. Therefore, we must reject the lies Satan has planted in our minds about the nature and character of God.

This chart helps us see how an incorrect perception of God can be changed to a true and accurate view of Him:

THE WAY YOU MAY HAVE PERCEIVED GOD

Situations
Various interactions with your father

Category
Your beliefs about all fathers

Thoughts
God is like my father; therefore, I will relate to Him in the same way that I relate to my father.

Emotions
Depending on the model of your relationship with your father, emotions about God may be love or anger, dependence or distrust, affection or fear.

Actions
Depending on the model of your relationship with your father, either: obedience, trust, and service *or* anger, rebellion, and withdrawal.

AN ACCURATE PERCEPTION OF GOD

Situations
Truths and biblical accounts about the activities of God

Category
Beliefs about God

Thoughts
God is loving, kind, and powerful. He is glad that I am His child.

Emotions
Comfort, thankfulness, joy, security, significance, contrition, humility, freedom, zeal, etc.

Actions
Obedience, trust, seeking His will, service, loving others, evangelism, discipleship, etc.

Aspects of a person's poor relationship with God can be traced back to false beliefs he has held about Him. For example:

Situation
I have been released by my employer.

False Belief
God punishes by making bad things happen to people.

Thought
God has decided I need to be punished.

Emotion
There's no way to please or understand Him. He's just like my father. I could never please him either!

Action
I've just got to have someone hold me and tell me they love me...or...I've got to prove myself in my next job...or...I need to escape the pain through alcohol, drugs, sex, or passivity.

Do you see the way our beliefs are embedded in our thoughts, and how they control our emotions? In turn, our emotions direct us to act in certain ways. If Satan has convinced us to believe his lies about God, we will find ourselves imprisoned by them.

Faith in the character of God enables us to live above the crises caused by circumstances. Identifying false beliefs about the character of God is, therefore, the first step toward new freedom in Christ Jesus.

Most of our painful emotions are actually signals which help us uncover deceptions in our belief system. Fear, anger, depression, and stress are some of the results of believing Satan's lies. When we begin to feel these emotions, we must ask, "What lie am I believing in this situation?"

In his book, *The Search for Significance*, Robert McGee explains that in almost every case we can trace our painful emotions back to one of four false beliefs. These deceptions distort our perceptions of the intimate love, forgiveness, and power of God, and keep us in a constant state of insecurity and turmoil.

The chart on the following pages contains not only the four foundational lies (or false beliefs), but also a list of some of the consequences of believing those lies. The chart then gives the contrast to the lies: God's specific Scriptural solutions and some of the results of living by these truths. [1]

False Beliefs

•*I must meet certain standards to feel good about myself.*
•*I must have the approval of certain others to feel good about myself.*
•*Those who fail are unworthy of love and deserve to be punished.*
•*I am what I am.*
•*I cannot change.*
•*I am hopeless.*

Consequences of False Beliefs

•Fear of failure; perfectionism; intensity about your own success; withdrawal from risks; manipulation of others to help you succeed.

•Fear of rejection; pleasing others at any cost; sensitivity to criticism; withdrawal to avoid disapproval.

•Fear of punishment; punishing others; blaming others when you fail; dry spiritual life.

•Feelings of inferiority; destructive habits; hopelessness.

God's Specific Solution

Because of *justification*, we are completely forgiven and fully pleasing to God. We no longer have to fear failure.

Because of *reconciliation*, we are totally accepted by God. We no longer have to fear rejection.

Because of *propitiation*, we are deeply loved by God. We no longer have to fear punishment or punish others.

Because of *regeneration*, we have been made new, complete in Christ. We no longer need to experience the pain of shame.

Results of God's Solution

•Freedom from the fear of failure; intensity about the right things–Christ and His Kingdom; love for Christ.

•Freedom from the fear of rejection; willingness to be open and vulnerable; able to relax around others; willingness to take criticism; desire to please God no matter what others think.

•Freedom from the fear of punishment; patience and kindness toward others; being quick to forgive; deep love for Christ.

•Christ-centered self-confidence; joy, courage, peace; desire to know Christ.

Why do we so easily believe lies about God? Why can't we recognize them for what they are? The reason may be that our beliefs are a mixture of both truth and deception, and until we see the contrast between them, most of us won't be astute enough to separate the two. In the previous example of being released by an employer, it is true that the person was fired, but to believe that the employer's decision was caused by God's cruelty is a wrong perception. Therefore, the person was believing both truth and deception at the same time.

False beliefs are not benign. They result in depression, fear, anger, or hopelessness.

As a corollary to the four false beliefs, Satan's next best weapon is encouraging us to question God's intentions in our lives. Here are some of his distortions of God's desires for us:

Distortion: Evil Comes from God

We hear about a good, righteous man being brutally murdered. We ask, "God, why did you let this happen?"

Did God care that this tragedy happened? Yes! But God did not cause the murder. A man out of control caused the tragedy. In a fallen world, many bad things–even tragic or evil things–happen. This is the nature of sin. It always produces heartache and pain. God does not snatch people from the fallen world the moment they become Christians. He leaves us here, in the midst of pain and suffering, to be light and salt to the rest of the fallen race.

Does God know about such suffering? Does He care? How does He react? We need only think of Jesus on the mount overlooking Jerusalem, weeping over the result of evil in that city. Or we may watch Him weeping at the tomb of his dear friend, Lazarus. Our God is One of compassion. His heart breaks when sin smashes lives.

How deceitful Satan is! I Pet. 5:8 tells us that he goes about *"like a roaring lion, seeking someone to devour."* At the very moment he infests men with murderous intent, he tries to make us think God is the cause!

When we hear about a tragic accident or the serious illness of a child, Satan wants us to blame God.

What does Scripture say about this?

> *When tempted, no one should say, "God is tempting me." For God cannot be tempted by evil, nor does he tempt anyone; but each one is tempted when, by his own evil desire, he is dragged away and enticed. Then, after desire has conceived, it gives birth to sin; and sin, when it is full-grown, gives birth to death. Don't be deceived, my dear brothers. Every good and perfect gift is from above, coming down from the Father of the heavenly lights, who does not change like shifting shadows. He chose to give us birth through the word of truth, that we might be a kind of firstfruits of all he created.*
>
> James 1:13-18

God may test us to strengthen our faith, but He never tempts us, because the goal of temptation is to cause a person to sin. God gives good and perfect gifts. He not only prospers us in tangible ways, but He gives us the strength and wisdom to endure difficulties. These, too, are good gifts!

What will we believe, Satan's lie or the Bible's clear explanation? If we believe that God is responsible for evil, we have distorted the truth. Who could trust a God like that? The Scriptures teach us that God is sovereign, but that doesn't mean He *always* reverses the effects of a fallen world. It does mean that He has a purpose even in the midst of our fallen world.

We must always remember that God is a Person, not just a powerful machine. Scripture repeatedly portrays Him as One who loves, who cares, who sorrows, who listens attentively. There is no evil in Him.

Distortion: God Doesn't Care About Me

God is often praised for nothing and blamed for everything. We make prayerless choices, sometimes knowing they are not what He wants for us. Yet, when things turn out badly, we ask, *God, if you really loved me, why didn't You keep me from doing that?*

The obvious solution is to recognize that God does not force us to follow Him. But he has built natural consequences into the spiritual realm, even as He has built physical laws into the universe. As certain as the law of gravity is the spiritual law that says, "What a man sows, he will reap."

With open arms, He reaches out toward us. He offers us full access to His wisdom and power if we will follow Him. At the same time, He is not a vending machine to supply all our whims and wants. As a Father, there are times when He knows it is best to say no to His child, and sometimes, He says, "wait." Regardless of His response, we can be assured that we will always receive His best when we leave the choices up to Him!

Perhaps a passive or absent or insensitive father modeled to you that fathers don't really care about their children, and that children just need to do the best they can on their own. But our Heavenly Father isn't like that! The Scriptures teach that He is loving, compassionate, and protective of His children.

Distortion: My Trials Don't Benefit Me

A very familiar passage to most of us, Rom. 8:28 says,

God causes all things to work together for good to those who love God, to those who are called according to His purpose.

This promise is often misunderstood to say that we will be perfectly happy with the outcome of our difficulties. But it doesn't say that. The verse talks about *His* purpose, not ours. Often, our purposes are self-serving. God's design is to wean us from our self-serving purposes to a life of devotion and service to Him. Our trials may not benefit us in the way we want them to, but they will benefit us in the way *He* wants them to.

Distortion: God Doesn't Meet Our Needs As We Expected

Satan whispers in our ear, "No wonder God has so few friends; He treats the ones He has so shabbily." With His complete knowledge of the present and future, the Lord often acts in ways we don't thoroughly understand. We fail to remember that our knowledge is limited. Our lack of information often prompts us to question the care and the provision of God.

Paul had a physical malady which caused him much distress. Three times he asked God to remove it. But the Lord had other plans. Paul recounted:

> *And He said to me, "My grace is sufficient for you, for power is perfected in weakness." Most gladly, therefore, I will rather boast about my weaknesses, that the power of Christ may dwell in me.*
>
> II Cor. 12:9

The Lord didn't do what Paul expected, but He met Paul's need nonetheless. And Paul responded with contentment and faith:

> *Therefore I am well content with weaknesses, with insults, with distresses, with persecutions, with difficulties, for Christ's sake; for when I am weak, then I am strong.*
>
> II Cor. 12:10

The Lord is powerful and compassionate. He can meet our needs, but sometimes His perception of our needs is different from ours. In His view, we may need courage, wisdom, and faith more than money, praise, and health. He will provide what we need, when we need it.

Distortion: God Should Have Made Me More Attractive

We ask, *How can I trust God when He has created me with this body and face?* Madison Avenue would have us believe that our appearance must be perfect if we are to experience true happiness and fulfillment. But comparison does not bring happiness and fulfillment, only pain and emptiness. Paul warned the Corinthians not to play that destructive game:

> *We do not dare to classify or compare ourselves with some who*
> *commend themselves. When they measure themselves by*
> *themselves and compare themselves with themselves, they are not*
> *wise.*   II Cor. 10:12

As long as we compare ourselves to someone else, we are foolish, forgetting that our worth is not based on how we look, but only on the love, forgiveness, and acceptance of God. We need to accept who we are as a gift from the Lord, and let Him show us how our appearance fits into His overall plan for our lives.

If we allow the Holy Spirit to replace lies and distortions with the truth about the character of God and our new identity in Christ, we will discover that we no longer need to be controlled by circumstances. Further, these circumstances will have less influence on our emotions. Our emotions are based on our *beliefs* about a situation, *not the situation* itself.

For example, Susan was told by her fiance, Jim, that their engagement was ended. She became deeply depressed. Her emotions were a direct result of her beliefs about the situation, not the situation itself. Let's consider two ways she might respond. First, a pattern that is based on a distorted view of God and herself:

Situation
Jim has broken their engagement.

Belief
God didn't create me as a beautiful
woman; He made me ugly.

Thought
I'm not capable of attracting a husband. My mother always made fun of the way I looked. I guess she was right.

Emotion
Anger at her mother as she remembers the ridicule; anger at Jim for destroying her dream of being loved and accepted; anger at God because He made her with such an ugly appearance.

Action
Repressed anger, depression, withdrawal, self-condemnation.

Susan doesn't have to come to these conclusions! She has a distorted view of God and blames Him for the breakup. She has isolated herself from the One who should be her greatest comfort and her closest companion. Her problem is not really the situation. Instead, it's the way she has perceived it and responded to it. She believes that God deliberately chooses "ugliness" for some people and forces them to be unattractive. But she can respond with faith and hope if she believes the truth about the character of God:

Situation
Jim has broken their engagement.

Belief
*Even though this hurts, I know that God loves me
and gives His best to me.*

Thought
I can learn to be content in the Lord while I am single.
or
I'm being guided to the husband He has for me.

Emotion

Oh God, this hurts so much! I really wanted to marry Jim
and have a loving and affirming husband, but thank You, Lord
for keeping me from marrying the wrong person.
Thank You that You are my constant companion.

Action

Honest expression of emotions to the Lord.
Appropriate expression of emotions to other people.
Developing and enjoying other friendships.
Thankfulness.

Susan can live with inner peace by trusting in the character of God, instead of living in anxiety and nursing her hurt. Satan's lie brings depression, but God's truth produces rest! She can experience what matters most in life: she is deeply loved by God, completely forgiven, fully pleasing, totally accepted, and complete in Christ. She can live a life of love and depth and meaning.

As we learn to identify the deceptions in our belief system, and discover in Scripture who God truly is, we can move into a totally new lifestyle. He has sent His Holy Spirit and loving, mature believers to guide us on our journey. All that we need has been provided.

[1]Robert McGee, *The Search For Significance* (Houston, TX: Rapha Publishing, 1987), pp. 102,103.

Ten

DEALING WITH FEARS

Learning facts in a classroom seldom does as much good as learning them in real-life situations. Just as you learned about your earthly father by watching him and interacting with him in all kinds of circumstances, so you can also learn about your Heavenly Father as you respond to Him and see Him at work in any and every situation. Many of life's situations produce anxiety, a form of fear. Such moments are the best times to discover why you are fearful and anxious. You can then learn to replace those fears with an understanding of the character of God and its result: faith, obedience, and peace.

We have already learned about the Four False Beliefs in Chapter Nine. Let's take another look at their consequences:

The Fear of Failure

Are you overly sensitive to criticism? Are you compelled to justify and explain your mistakes? Do you become depressed when you fail? Do you become angry with people who interfere with your attempts to succeed, and who make you feel incompetent? This fear of failure is the consequence of the false belief: *I must meet certain standards in order to feel good about myself.*

The Fear of Rejection

Do you go out of your way to be liked by people, even when you must compromise your convictions? Do you avoid certain people? Are you devastated when someone else gets more attention than you do? Do you daydream about promotions or compliments? Do you compare your looks, possessions, status, prestige, or abilities with others? The fear of rejection is the result of the false belief: *I must be approved by certain others to feel good about myself.*

The Fear of Punishment
and the Desire to Punish Others

Are you afraid to make a mistake because you fear that someone will criticize you? Do you fear what God might do to you? After you fail, do you feel like God is disgusted or angry with you? Do you condemn yourself when you fail as a type of self-punishment? How do you respond when others fail, especially when you were depending on them? Are you generally accepting or critical of others? Guilt and condemnation are the consequences of the false belief: *Those who fail (including myself) are unworthy of love and deserve to be punished.*

The Feeling of Shame

Do you like the way you look? Do you feel past experiences have ruined your life? Do you see yourself as a "loser," and often feel inferior when you are with a group of friends? This leads to the false belief: *I am what I am. I cannot change. I am hopeless.*

Your Fears Can Help You Experience
God's Love and Acceptance

You can actually use these fears to learn more about God's character. For example, Ronald has just overheard two secretaries in his office gossiping about him. One has said, "He looks like a wilted flower. He never has his suits pressed. He's a mess!" Ronald is heart-broken! He is shattered by their criticism.

Ronald's father was always critical of him. He still remembers a time when, as a small boy, he had earned enough money by mowing lawns to purchase a pocket knife. When he proudly showed it to his dad, he was rebuffed: "You're stupid to waste money on a knife, Ron. You should have put that money in the bank. Some day you're going to go to college, and that takes a lot of cash. If you had a lick of sense, you'd be saving for it right now!"

Ronald has been learning that his perception of God has been shaped by his earthly father's conduct. In the past, he never realized how his responses to situations reflected his view of God. Now, in this situation, he was determined not to be devastated by petty gossip. He closed his office door and read Col. 1:19-22:

> *For God was pleased to have all his fullness dwell in him, and through him to reconcile to himself all things, whether things on earth or things in heaven, by making peace through his blood, shed on the cross. Once you were alienated from God and were enemies in your minds because of your evil behavior. But now he has reconciled you by Christ's physical body through death to present you holy in his sight, without blemish and free from accusation...*

As Ronald thought about these verses, he began to feel a sense of peace. His worth did not depend upon the petty gossip of the secretaries, but was based on the unconditional love, forgiveness, and acceptance of God. He had been working long hours, and it was true that his clothes needed pressing, but what did it matter?

Ronald closed his Bible and began to pray:

> *Father, You completely understand me and You love and accept me unconditionally. When my heart cries out for someone to care enough to take time to understand, I'll remember that You understand.*
>
> *Father, those times I thought you were distant and insensitive, I was deceived. There is not one minute that passes when You are not sensitive to every detail of my life.*

He then took a pen and began to jot down his thoughts. Glancing over them, he continued praying:

> *Father, allow me to recall those times when You have really understood: You were there for me when my wife faced serious surgery. You understood when I feared the plant would close, and I would lose my job. You understood when I flunked my C.P.A. exam and had to take it over.*

Ronald continued to jot some phrases on his pad and prayed:

> *Father, I remember the times when my dad put me down as a teenager. I decided then that I would stop going to church because I felt that if I got too close to You, that You would ridicule me, too. I was deceived then, and I believed that You really didn't understand me. Dear Father, I confess these thoughts are lies. I accept You for who You say You are. I thank You that Your love and acceptance overcomes the sense of rejection I have been feeling because of the criticism I just heard!*

Consider Using Ronald's Plan

1. *Realize* that you are experiencing anger, fear, or anxiety. Also realize which lie you are believing (see the chart in Chapter Nine).

2. *Reject* the lie because it is a deception which distorts your perception of God and produces painful consequences in your life.

3. *Replace* these deceptions with the truths of God's Word. Then reflect on these truths to see how they apply in your present situation. And finally, praise the Lord for His love, forgiveness, and power.

The plan is very simple, but it can prove to be profoundly helpful. You can turn every time of stress into a time of reflection, prayer, and praise.

Whenever you realize that you are being anxious over a situation, a comment, a thought, a problem, or a relationship, take time to use this plan. As the days pass, you will develop a habit of confronting every negative thought with the powerful and affirming truths of God's Word.

As you mature, your confidence in Him will give you a new way of dealing with stress. You will be increasingly controlled by the Holy Spirit of God, and you will begin to discover the joy that comes from His control.

Eleven

"WHAT DO I DO
WITH MY EMOTIONS?"

When some people analyze the difference between the character of God and their parents, they experience instant understanding and relief. *Oh, so that's why I've felt distant from the Lord! Now I understand.* For them, the transition to a deep and fresh experience with the Lord is fairly easy.

But for others, this catharsis comes later. When they begin to recognize the contrast between the unconditional love of God and the neglect, abuse, or manipulation of their parents, they go through a period of great pain before they can experience relief. Years of repressed emotions can't be brushed aside or solved easily and quickly.

A few years ago, I met a young pastor, Chris, who was very shy, but also very responsible and hard working. He was bright and athletic. I wondered why he seemed to feel awkward in social situations. We had opportunities to talk on several occasions, and I began to ask him some questions about his background:

"Chris, what are your parents like?"

"They're okay, I guess. Dad's an engineer and Mom's a high school English teacher."

"How did you get along with them when you were growing up?"

"Fine, I guess."

"How did they treat you? Did you feel loved and accepted?"

After a long pause, Chris looked down and said, "I guess I was kind of the ugly duckling in the family. My brothers and my sister were smart and did well in sports, but I came along last and, well, I guess I didn't do as well as they wanted me to."

"How do you know that, Chris?"

"No matter how hard I tried, I never could do all they wanted me to do." His voice got lower. "I just wasn't the son that I should have been."

"Did you think it was up to you to make your parents happy?"

"Of course! If I had been the kind of son I should have been–like my brothers–they would have been happy."

"How did they show you that they loved you?"

"My father, well...he....I don't think he did very much. He provided for me, but he isn't a very loving man–at least not to me. My mother would tell me that I'd done well in sports or in school, but when my father shouted at me, she never defended me or anything." He concluded, "It's my fault. I just wasn't the kind of son they could be proud of."

A sad story. I spent the next half-hour explaining to Chris that it wasn't his fault. It wasn't up to him to make his parents happy. That responsibility is on the parents, not the child. It is the God-given responsibility of parents to love and protect their children.

But Chris wouldn't buy it. The sense of guilt and responsibility was so ingrained in him that he couldn't see that he was a victim of a form of abuse. He showed no emotion at all during our conversation. He was numb.

After a couple of talks with Chris, he started to see the light. "You mean...they were supposed to love me unconditionally...and its not up to me to make them happy?"

"Yes. If they had loved you unconditionally, you would have responded in love and glad obedience to them, not guilt and fearful obedience."

Just then, Chris raised his arm and slammed his fist on the desk! His eyes widened and then he glared in anger. "I can't believe they did that to me! What would my life be like now if they had loved me?"

It was the beginning of the healing process for this young man, and after months of reflection and discussion and growth, he's doing much better.

The story about Chris is not an isolated one. When we get in touch with our past, it sometimes opens a Pandora's box of painful emotions. These emotions are chiefly anger and fear, with variations of each.

Anger may take the form of mild frustration, but if repressed over a period of time, it festers into resentment and bitterness. These feelings often find their outlet and expression in revenge. Or, a person may try to compensate by being driven as a workaholic, or by escaping as an alcoholic.

Fear is less volatile, but it is just as damaging. It causes numbness and withdrawal that can amount to emotional, spiritual, and social paralysis. Most people who have repressed emotions have some combination of anger and fear. The fears of rejection and failure can cause a myriad of painful symptoms.

There are three principles that will help us handle our emotions, whether they are mild or the harsh product of years of repression. These principles are:

1. Be honest.
2. Express yourself fully to God.
3. Express yourself appropriately to the other person.

Be Honest

The first step in coping with repressed emotions is, of course, to recognize that they are there. When one lady began to understand how her father's outbursts of anger had driven her into an emotional shell, she became angry at him. But she caught herself, "I can't be angry. I'm a Christian." She started to confess her anger to the Lord.

If she had stopped there, she would never have been able to deal effectively with her past. She would have continued to repress her emotions.

After some patient instruction, she realized that Christians don't just have happy feelings. They get angry, too! The emotion isn't always the result of their sin. The sin may be the neglect or abuse that others inflicted on them, and the anger or fear is just a response to that pain. Willful disobedience is sin, but emotions are the products of many factors including our sins, others' sins, other experiences, our background, hormones, etc. Emotions, in and of themselves, are not sin.

The correct response when we realize that we are angry or fearful is to be honest about our emotion, try to understand its root cause, and then choose to act in a way that honors the Lord.

Sometimes I hear a Christian say, "I'm really frustrated!" Often this statement is another way to avoid saying that we are angry because anger is somehow not as acceptable as frustration. It is an attempt to downplay our emotions and to rationalize the severity of them. A friend of mine used to say "I'm frustrated!" fairly often. When I realized that there was more emotion there than mild frustration, I decided to ask him, "Rick, aren't you a little more than 'frustrated'? Aren't you really angry?"

He looked at me for a moment, then a big smile spread across his face. "Yes, you're right. I guess I am mad. It just doesn't sound spiritual for me to say I'm angry."

We rationalize a lot of anger by saying that we're "frustrated." We need to be honest so that we can analyze the source of our anger and find a healing solution from the Lord.

Express Yourself Fully to God

The Lord is never surprised by our emotions. He is omniscient. He knew everything about us before the world was created. And He is our understanding, loving, and trustworthy confidant. We can tell Him everything about how we think and feel—and we should tell Him.

David wrote this admonition to us:

> *Trust in Him at all times, O people; pour out your heart before Him; God is a refuge for us.*
>
> Ps. 62:8

"Pour out your heart" to the Lord. One man I know is deeply emotional. When he feels something, he feels it deeply! On a few occasions, when he has been really upset, he has gotten into his car and driven down the highway screaming at the top of his lungs! I'm not sure what the other motorists have thought, but he says that this enables him to tell the Lord how angry he feels without any inhibitions.

Few of us will go to this extreme (The highways are crazy enough as it is!), but all of us need to express our thoughts and emotions to the Lord. And that takes time. A couple of minutes won't do it. We need to get into the habit of both instant honesty, and quiet, prolonged communication with the Lord so that we can reflect on our feelings and situations and His truth about them.

David was an excellent model of "pouring out your heart to the Lord." The Psalms reflect his deeply personal relationship with God, and include a full range of emotions. Let's take a look at a small sample of David's honesty with the Lord:

Fear
Psalm 140:1-4

Rescue me, O Lord, from evil men; preserve me from violent men, who devise evil things in their hearts; they continually stir up wars. They sharpen their tongues as a serpent; poison of a viper is under their lips. Keep me, O Lord, from the hands of the wicked; preserve me from violent men, who have purposed to trip up my feet.

Joy
Psalm 140:6-7

I said to the Lord, "Thou art my God; give ear, O Lord, to the voice of my supplications. O God the Lord, the strength of my salvation, Thou hast covered my head in the day of battle."

Confidence
Psalm 140:12-13

I know that the Lord will maintain the cause of the afflicted, and justice for the poor. Surely the righteous will give thanks to Thy name; the upright will dwell in Thy presence.

Anger
Psalm 139:19-22

O that Thou wouldst slay the wicked, O God; depart from me, therefore, men of bloodshed. For they speak against Thee wickedly, and Thine enemies take Thy name in vain. Do I not hate those who hate Thee, O Lord? And do I not loathe those who rise up against Thee? I hate them with the utmost hatred; they have become my enemies.

Anxiety
Psalm 141:1

O Lord, I call upon Thee; hasten to me! Give ear to my voice when I call to Thee!

As you express yourself fully to the Lord, remember to listen to Him, too, as His Spirit reminds you of passages of Scripture and prompts you to think about Him and His desires for you. Remember to focus on His character, His promises, and His commands so that you can understand how he wants you to respond to your circumstances.

Express Yourself Appropriately to the Person

After you have expressed yourself fully to God, you will need to express yourself appropriately to the other person. But you don't need to tell him everything you have thought about him! That should be reserved for the time when you pour out your heart to the Lord.

But what should you say? The answer to that question comes from another question: what will help that person? The goal of expressing yourself is to benefit the other person. Loving confrontation can be a stepping stone for that person's growth and maturity, and ultimately, it can greatly strengthen your relationship with him.

Think about that person's maturity level and his ability to apply what you would say. A reproof that would be digestible to a mature person may devastate a weaker one. You will need God's wisdom to know how much to say, and just as importantly, how much not to say. Solomon wrote:

A prudent man conceals knowledge, but the heart of fools proclaims folly.

Prov. 12:23

A wise man won't tell everything he knows, but a fool will tell everything, no matter how much it hurts the other person.

On rare occasions, the best thing to tell the other person is nothing. Do you remember Chris, the young pastor we described at the beginning of this chapter? What would be appropriate for him to say to his parents? After careful consultation, we realized that his parents wouldn't understand Chris, no matter how carefully he expressed himself. He decided to act lovingly toward them even though he would no longer bow to their manipulative condemnation. His new attitude and actions may result in their greater condemnation of him, or possibly, questions about his changed life. The latter situation, Chris decided, would provide for a more teachable moment.

When a person begins to get in touch with repressed emotions, those emotions may seem almost unbearable. But continued repression is not the solution.

When a person contracts a terminal disease like cancer, he usually goes through several stages of emotional responses. Elisabeth Kübler-Ross described these stages in her very helpful book, *On Death and Dying*. Those with severe emotional trauma go through similar stages, including: denial, bargaining, anger, acceptance, and grief.

Many people at first deny the pain of neglect, abuse, or manipulation. They either suppress the pain and pretend it isn't there, or they blame themselves, assuming that problems are their fault.

When the problem *is* finally confronted and the repressed emotions begin to flow, we often try to bargain with God or with that person. We ask, in effect, *How can I get that person to love me? What can I do to be accepted? I'll change! I'll do anything!*

But sooner or later, we realize that bargaining won't work. We haven't been able to win their approval in the past, and we can't win it now. Then, we will often experience deep anger toward the one who caused the pain. At that point, the anger should not be repressed again. It needs to be, as we have seen, fully expressed to God. This stage of anger may last for several months.

After the anger is expressed and experienced, a stage of grief often follows. This experience of a sense of loss is very positive and healthy. The past cannot be relived. A life has been damaged, but now there is a healthy grief over the loss, not destructive anger. When the sense of grief has been fully felt, a catharsis occurs. There is relief and acceptance. Life can go on.

This process doesn't happen overnight. Some people may take a prolonged period of time just to uncork the emotions and move from denial to the anger stage. The time frame isn't as important as the process itself. Be patient and expect the process to take its course. If you try to hurry, you'll be disappointed and possibly experience even more pain because of unrealistic expectations. But if you are patient, the messy and painful emotions will be experienced, and God will provide healing and hope.

We need to be honest about those emotions no matter how painful they may be. We need to fully express our thoughts and feelings to God, and express ourselves appropriately to other people. That will ultimately bring healing to both ourselves and others.

Twelve

RIVERS IN THE DESERT

When you think about your relationship with your parents, what thoughts and emotions emerge: pain or thankfulness, cursing or blessing, or some combination of the two? Has it occurred to you that God can use even the most neglectful or abusive parents to produce strengths in your life?

No, the pain of not being loved, accepted, and protected as a child is not God's primary design for a family, but He can use our difficulties to produce good. Most of us love to quote Rom. 8:28:

And we know that God causes all things to work together for good to those who love God, to those who are called according to His purpose.

We need to apply this promise in this most sensitive of situations: our relationships with our parents.

Before we look at the various strengths that God can build through the ordeal of a painful childhood, we need to again ask the question, *Why? Why did God let this happen in my life? Couldn't a loving God have given me strong, loving parents?*

The role of suffering is a complex and delicate issue with extreme positions taken by some people. We need to understand that our sovereign God has allowed (not caused) evil in the world. Let's examine three causes of suffering: the fallen nature of man, the consequences of sin, and the Lord's work of pruning for greater fruitfulness.

When Adam and Eve sinned, man's perfection ceased. Mankind and all of creation fell from perfect union with God. When a person enters this world, he enters a world that is dominated by the prince of evil...

> *...in which you formerly walked according to the course of this world, according to the prince of the power of the air, of the spirit that is now working in the sons of disobedience.*
>
> Eph. 2:2

Apart from Christ, mankind is subject to the unrestrained passions and pains of sin. Children, unfortunately, suffer greatly from this predicament. Too often, God's plan for the family to model His love and power is effectively nullified.

The cross of Christ enables fallen man to be reconciled to God, but we are not immediately extricated from this fallen world. It is our responsibility and privilege to represent Him to others who are fallen and desperately in need of His grace. As we represent Him, however, we are still affected by the fallen and evil forces in the world. Even many Christian parents fail to accurately represent the character of God to their children. Instead of protecting and providing a godly example, they model the same selfishness, possessiveness, or neglect as their heathen neighbors.

The consequences of personal sin cause a great deal of suffering. Gal. 6:7-8 states:

> *Do not be deceived, God is not mocked; for whatever a man sows, this he will also reap. For the one who sows to his own flesh shall from the flesh reap corruption, but the one who sows to the Spirit shall from the Spirit reap eternal life.*

On television we see happy endings at the end of almost every program, no matter how grave the problems of the characters may be. This provides a very misleading picture of real life. These shows don't describe the tremendous and prolonged pain of adultery, alcoholism, selfishness, jealousy, and hatred. That wouldn't sell detergent!

The truth is that these sins destroy families, create deep bitterness, and crush the lives of those who are most vulnerable: the children.

A third cause of suffering (and we could list several others) is pruning. This kind of suffering differs from the other two because it is not the result of sin, but is the result of honoring Christ. Christ used the metaphor of a vineyard to describe this phenomenon:

> *Every branch in Me that does not bear fruit, He takes away; and every branch that bears fruit, He prunes it, that it may bear more fruit.* John 15:2

> *I am the vine, you are the branches; he who abides in Me, and I in him, he bears much fruit; for apart from Me you can do nothing.* John 15:5

If we are serious about honoring Christ, we will bear fruit. And if we bear fruit, Christ says that He will prune us so that we can bear even more fruit. His purpose in this action is very positive, but it is painful!

Whether the cause of suffering is sin or fruitfulness, God can use our pain for good. Even when the pain is inflicted by a family member and the hurt is excruciating, God can still use it for good. Joseph's brothers wanted to murder their upstart little brother (Gen. 38:18-20), but one of them, Reuben, persuaded the others not to kill him. So his brothers sold him as a slave. After many years, and divine intervention, Joseph rose to prominence in Egypt. He became the prime minister under the Egyptian pharaoh.

His father and his brothers experienced a severe famine in Canaan and went to Egypt to buy food. When they came to Joseph, he could have had them executed on the spot, but he didn't. Joseph believed that God had a purpose for allowing him to suffer bitter rejection and brutal treatment by his own brothers. Instead of cursing them, he said to them:

> *"And as for you, you meant evil against me, but God meant it for good in order to bring about this present result, to preserve many people alive. So therefore, do not be afraid; I will provide for you and your little ones." So he comforted them and spoke kindly to them.* Gen. 50:20-21

Joseph did not see himself as a victim of injustice (even though he was!). He saw himself as an extension of God's care for his family–even though they had wanted to murder him. He believed that God had a purpose for his suffering, and this sense of purpose enabled him to see himself as a servant of God instead of as a victim.

Perhaps you have been a victim of neglect, abuse, or manipulation by your parents or family members. Do you see yourself only as a victim? Or do you see that God has a higher purpose, and that you can participate in that purpose as an extension of His love and power? A "victim mentality" limits our focus to our own pain and needs. Believing that God has a higher purpose enables us to take our eyes off of ourselves so that we can serve Him and help others.

Our pain probably won't magically evaporate as we focus on God's purposes, but we will have a new sense of contentment when we realize that God can turn even our greatest pain or weakness into strength. Paul described this phenomenon when he wrote:

> *And He has said to me, "My grace is sufficient for you, for power is perfected in weakness." Most gladly, therefore, I will rather boast about my weaknesses, that the power of Christ may dwell in me. Therefore I am well content with weaknesses, with insults, with distresses, with persecutions, with difficulties, for Christ's sake; for when I am weak, then I am strong.*
>
> II Cor. 12:9-10

The Lord can and will use your past to develop strengths in your life. Because of its difficulties, you will be able to understand people and help others more. Let's examine these strengths.

Compassion for Others

Have you ever been really hurting; become desperate enough to tell someone because you needed his help, and had him look at you strangely and say, "What's the matter with you? Why don't you just trust the Lord?" That helped a lot, didn't it!?!

Simplistic answers don't cut it for hurting people. But how does a person develop understanding and compassion? Usually by experiencing pain himself. Our ability to comfort others is more or less proportional to the degree that we have experienced comfort in our own times of pain. Paul wrote to the Corinthian believers:

Blessed be the God and Father of our Lord Jesus Christ, the Father of mercies and God of all comfort; who comforts us in all our affliction so that we may be able to comfort those who are in any affliction with the comfort with which we ourselves are comforted by God. For just as the sufferings of Christ are ours in abundance, so also our comfort is abundant though Christ.

II Cor. 1:3-5

A lady in our church, Mary, recently experienced the pain of her father's death. At the funeral was an array of expensive floral arrangements, and she received many sympathy cards, but she said that one note meant more to her than any other. It was from a friend whose mother had died of cancer several months before. She wrote of how her emotions had been torn and her sense of stability fractured. And she wrote about the comfort she had received. She didn't give advice. She didn't preach. She just let Mary know that she understood. That was the greatest comfort.

If you have experienced the pain of neglect, abuse, or manipulation, you will be able to understand and comfort others who are experiencing the pains of hurting families. God can use you deeply and profoundly in the lives of others.

Dependence on the Lord

When the prophet Samuel came to Jesse's house, he invited Jesse and his sons to a ceremonial sacrifice (I Samuel 16). It was an intense and exciting moment in Jesse's family. "Why has the prophet come to our home?" they undoubtedly wondered.

Samuel had been directed by the Lord to go to Jesse's home so that he could anoint a new king of Israel. "Bring your sons to me," Samuel instructed. One by one, Jesse's seven sons passed in front of the prophet, but the Lord said to Samuel, "No, not this one...not this one...not this one." There was no one left. "Are these all of your sons?" he asked.

Jesse replied, "There remains yet the youngest, and behold, he is tending the sheep."

Samuel ordered Jesse to bring David to him, and the Lord instructed, "Arise, anoint him; for this is he." David was to become the king of Israel, but his father didn't even count him among his own sons! Samuel had instructed Jesse to bring *all* of his sons to him, but Jesse had left David out in the field with the sheep. He was a reject in the eyes of his father.

His brothers, too, ridiculed David. (After all, that's how their father treated him.) When David took provisions to his brothers while they were in Saul's army, the eldest, Eliab, replied:

> *...Why have you come down? And with whom have you left those few sheep in the wilderness? I know your insolence and the wickedness of your heart; for you have come down in order to see the battle.* I Sam. 17:28

Rejected by his father, scorned by his brother, David spent many lonely nights watching the sheep. A deeply sensitive young man, he needed to be accepted. He needed to be understood. No one else cared about him—no one else but the Lord. So day after day and night after night, alone with the Lord while he was tending the sheep, David developed a close, rich relationship with God. His psalms reflect a depth of intimacy, honesty, and understanding probably unparalleled in history. Yet we may fail to recognize the crucible that developed this intimacy and dependence: rejection. David had no where else to turn, so he turned to the Lord.

Somehow, David recognized that God was not like his father. Maybe David memorized the Scriptures and realized that God is loving, kind and powerful instead of harsh, demeaning, and neglectful like Jesse was. David's understanding of the contrast between the Lord and his father enabled him to experience the love and power of God's presence.

Perhaps you have experienced rejection. Perhaps you have no one else to depend on but God. He is faithful and kind and powerful. You can depend on Him even if you can depend on no one else.

Perception

Children need love and acceptance to experience stability. Without these provisions, they have to fend for themselves. Some try to block the pain by building emotional walls. "If I can keep from getting close to others, then I won't get hurt," they surmise.

But others develop a different defense mechanism. They become acutely aware of the mood and intentions of those around them, and then change their behavior to win approval. Their "antennae" are always up, analyzing every word, expression and action. *Does that look mean that she's upset with me? Why did he raise his voice? His words say that he cares about me, but the tone of his voice tells me that he's faking it. What can I say to get her to like me?"* It's a cat and mouse game, and the children are the poor mice.

This ability to "read" others is a tremendous strength, even if it is learned through great anguish and painful introspection. Bill is a friend of mine who is the most perceptive person I know. His parents fought a lot when he was young. They were so involved in their own selfishness and bitterness that they often neglected him. His defense was to try to please them in every way he could so that they would notice him and approve of him. He learned to read their every mood.

Bill can sense the attitudes of others long before most people can. I often ask him how he thinks other people in the church are doing. I may sense that something isn't quite right, but Bill usually has it pinpointed, described, and illustrated with several examples.

He is so perceptive that I sometimes jokingly walk into his office and say, "Hi, Bill, how am I doing?" His sense of perception is a great strength, but it was through pain that he acquired it.

Have you learned to "read" others because you felt that you had to respond perfectly as a child to gain approval? Perception is a wonderful strength to have.

Reflective

Some people respond to perceived rejection by becoming very cautious. These people are characterized by the thought, *I have to be right before I act.* This fear of failure and rejection can paralyze, but it can also have the positive result of developing an ability to reflect. This strength is similar to that of perception, but centers more on ideas, problems, and issues than on people.

Patty is a friend of mine who has learned to analyze issues to a great degree. She will often ask a series of questions that no one else even thinks to ask. She likes to have her bases covered to avoid mistakes.

Some of us are risk-takers, blindly rushing ahead without being willing (or able) to take a hard look at the facts. We need someone like Patty who is more cautious and who will ask the hard questions.

Are you a cautious person? Do you analyze problems well? Are you so cautious that you are afraid to make a decision even when all the questions have been answered? Or is your reflection a strength that enables you to ask the questions, get the solutions, and press on with a high degree of success?

Effectiveness

Lyle was from an alcoholic family. He received very little attention, and what attention he did receive was often condemnation. Like anyone else, he developed a defense mechanism to blunt the pain. His defense mechanism was to excel in school and in sports. He was driven to do well because he thought that good grades and athletics would earn the respect and approval that he longed for.

But no matter how well he performed (he was an honor student and an all-star in three sports), he still felt like an outcast from his family. When he made 95 on an exam, his mother asked him why he didn't make

100. When he went 4 for 4 on his baseball team, it still wasn't enough to win his parents' approval.

When Lyle graduated from college, he focused his finely-tuned skills toward the business world. Soon, he became a vice-president, the best employee in the company. He made a lot of money, married a beautiful girl, and continued to advance in his career. *Maybe if I get to the next position,* he reasoned, *they'll approve of me.* But they didn't.

Some people, like Lyle, have learned how to effectively focus their attention and abilities to accomplish almost any given task. Are you exceptionally effective, but feel like nothing you do is ever quite good enough? Have you experienced the unconditional love and acceptance of God so that your drive to be effective can be channelled for the Lord's glory and for His purposes?

When we are in the midst of the agony of rejection, it is often difficult to see the strengths that God is building in us. We just want relief! Yet God is there, building and developing strengths in us that will enable us to honor Him and help others. It is encouraging that, no matter how difficult your past has been, God has a divine purpose for you, and He will use those very difficulties to develop depth, character, and skills so that you can have a great impact on other people. He can produce hope out of despair, compassion out of pain, joy out of bitterness, and strength out of weakness. Isaiah wrote:

> *Behold, I will do something new, now it will spring forth; will you not be aware of it? I will even make a roadway in the wilderness, rivers in the desert.* Is. 43:19

Thirteen

BREAKING THE CYCLE:

Modeling God's Character To Your Children

There is a startling and disturbing dictum in the Bible. It says that sin is reproduced in a family for four generations!

> *And the Lord descended in the cloud and stood there with him as he called upon the name of the Lord. Then the Lord passed by in front of him and proclaimed, "The Lord, the Lord God, compassionate and gracious, slow to anger, and abounding in lovingkindness and truth; who keeps lovingkindness for thousands, who forgives iniquity, transgression and sin; yet He will by no means leave the guilty unpunished, visiting the iniquity of fathers on the children and on the grandchildren to the third and fourth generations." And Moses made haste to bow low toward the earth and worship.* Ex. 34:5-8

The bitterness, anger, neglect, abuse, passivity, and manipulation of a father will be passed down to his children, his grandchildren, and his great-grandchildren. That may seem harsh and cruel, but it is an accurate reflection of the terrible consequences of sin.

Is this statement, given to Moses about 3500 years ago, still in effect today? I talked with a man, Steve, who described how his father very rarely showed affection for him:

"Dad was a driver. He worked long and hard, and he expected his children to do the same. I can remember that if I didn't do some job exactly like he wanted it—which was pretty often, though I tried really hard to do a good job—he let me have it. He chewed me out. I remember only one time that he put his hand on my shoulder when I was growing up. But he put his hand on my backside a few more times than that!"

I asked, "Steve, did you ever spend much time with his father, your granddad?"

He instantly responded with a look of new revelation: "You know, I did, and he was a crotchety, old goat. He seemed to always have something to say about everybody, and it wasn't very complimentary! He even gave his grandchildren a pretty rough time."

Steve went on to say, "And I don't want to admit it, but I treat my children the same way my father treated me; the same way his father treated him. I hate it! And I feel so guilty about it!"

The sins of Steve's grandfather were being reproduced in his son, his grandson (Steve), and even his great-grandchildren.

Can this cycle be broken? Can the destruction and pain of reproduced sin be stopped? By the grace and power of God, yes, it can. Prov. 28:13 describes the process:

> *He who conceals his transgressions will not prosper, but he who confesses and forsakes them will find compassion.*

Most people try to conceal their transgressions by either denying that their actions are wrong, or else feeling so guilty for them that they can't face them. To break the cycle of sin, we must bring them out into the light of God's Word with the confidence of His forgiveness.

To confess means "to agree with." When we confess our sins, we agree with God that our attitude and action is, indeed, sin. Sin is not just relegated to the more blatant varieties: murder, rape, and stealing. Sin is an attitude which says to God, *I want to run my own life. You go Your way; I'll go mine.* At its most fundamental level, sin is selfishness, and it can be expressed in a host of both subtle and blatant ways.

Confession also involves agreeing with God that Christ's death is the complete payment for sin; therefore, we are completely forgiven.

But there is a third step we must take after agreeing both that we have sinned, and that Christ's death has paid the penalty for that sin so that we are forgiven. The third step is to forsake that sin. To forsake means "to renounce, to leave altogether, to desert, and to abandon." It means that we go to any length to reject that attitude or behavior and replace it with an attitude or behavior that is honoring to Christ.

Paul describes this process of rejecting sin and replacing it with godliness in his letter to the Ephesian believers:

> *But you did not learn Christ in this way, if indeed you have heard*
> *Him and have been taught in Him, just as truth is in Jesus, that, in*
> *reference to your former manner of life, you lay aside the old self,*
> *which is being corrupted in accordance with the lusts of deceit,*
> *and that you be renewed in the spirit of your mind, and put on the*
> *new self, which in the likeness of God has been created in*
> *righteousness and holiness of the truth.*
>
> Eph. 4:20-24

He instructs us to *"lay aside the old self, which is being corrupted in accordance with the lusts of deceit."* "Laying aside" is a parallel of confession. To lay something aside, you first have to recognize that it is there and realize that it is harmful to you and to others.

Being *"renewed in the spirit of* [our] *minds"* occurs as we reflect on the truth of the Scriptures–especially the deep implications of the Gospel– that we are deeply loved, completely forgiven, fully pleasing, and totally accepted by God because of the cross of Christ.

"Putting on the new self" means that we make active choices to spend time and effort doing those things that honor the Lord and encourage others.

This process doesn't occur by magic. Breaking the cycle of reproduced family sin doesn't happen by waving a wand or reading a verse. It takes a combination of powerful, God-given forces. The Scriptures are the only source of truth about God, about ourselves, and about the process of restoration that God can perform in our lives. The Holy Spirit is the agent of change. Self-effort is not enough. It takes the transforming power of the Spirit of God to produce real, long-lasting change in a person's life. The body of Christ needs to play its role, both corporately and individually, of modeling and affirming the truth of the

Scriptures and the work of God's Spirit. And finally, God has given each of us a will so that we can play our role in the process. It is our choice to depend either on ourselves or on Christ to produce change. It is our choice to either continue living out the reproduced sin pattern in our family history, or to have the courage to begin acting in a way that honors Christ and helps our children, even though it seems that every fiber of our hearts and emotions is tugging at us to continue that destructive cycle. If all of these steps are in operation, then the transformation that we long for will eventually and gradually happen!

Yes, there is hope for change and restoration, even if you have miserably failed to model the character of God to your children. There is hope in the prophet Joel's words:

> *And the threshing floors will be full of grain, and the vats will overflow with the new wine and oil. Then I will make up to you for the years that the swarming locust has eaten, the creeping locust, the stripping locust, and the gnawing locust, my great army which I sent among you. And you shall have plenty to eat and be satisfied, and praise the name of the Lord your God, who has dealt wondrously with you; then My people will never be put to shame.*
> Joel 2:24-26

We can apply this promise to our need of changing in the way we treat our children: *"I will make up to you for the years that the swarming locust has eaten."*

Charles Swindoll wrote in his book, *You And Your Child:*

> *The locust of parental neglect and insensitivity may have taken its toll on your children's lives years ago. The swarming insects of indifference or ignorance or impatience or a host of other famines brought on by your failures ate away at your relationship with those precious children, resulting today in barrenness and perhaps even bitterness and resentment on their part.*
> *Now they are grown. You cannot relive those years. That's a fact. But God can renew them. That's a promise. That's hope!* [1]

Lets look at five principles that are stepping stones for learning to model the character of God to our children. These stepping stones of change include:

1. A changed self-concept
2. A changed purpose
3. Changed affections
4. A changed schedule
5. Changed actions

A Changed Self-Concept

As we have mentioned several times in this book, the way most people try to gain their security and significance is through their performance and the approval of others. But this is a hopeless rat race because God has created us in such a way that only His love, forgiveness, and acceptance can truly satisfy us.

We need to change the way we see ourselves. If we are driven to perform, we may use others and then condemn them when they fail. If we seek the approval of others, we may alter our behavior to suit them, without being ourselves at all. Or, we may use *our* approval as a tool to manipulate others to make us happy.

Robin is a young mother who quickly realized that her perception of herself radically affects how she treats her children. As she has become more and more convinced that she is unconditionally loved by God, she has become more patient and affectionate with her children.

A Changed Purpose

Our culture glorifies the triad of selfish purposes: success, pleasure, and approval. Practically every commercial on television, every billboard, and every magazine ad tells us that their product or service will give us success, pleasure, or the approval of others. Then we'll be really happy! (Hogwash!)

Dan Hayes, traveling speaker for Campus Crusade for Christ, illustrates this purpose by describing this dialogue:

Q: "What do most people want out of life?"

A: "They want the American dream: a nice car, a nice home, a nice job, a nice boat, nice vacations, nice neighbors, a nice husband or a nice wife, and nice children."

They work like crazy to get these things, but after a while, they get bored with them.

Q: "Then what do they want?"

A: "They want a bigger car, a bigger house, a better job, better vacations, better neighbors, bigger and better children, and a better spouse. People are never satisfied with 'things'!"

In fact, God has made us so that these things *cannot* satisfy us. No matter how we pursue them, they leave us empty. Jeremiah wrote about the emptiness of pursuing selfish goals with the vain hope that they will satisfy us:

> *For My people have committed two evils: They have forsaken Me, the fountain of living waters, to hew for themselves cisterns, broken cisterns, that can hold no water.*
>
> Jer. 2:13

Most people never even think about their purpose in life. They just adopt whatever purpose is given to them by someone else. Many companies demand that their employees put the company at the top of their priority list. One electronic company in the Southwest told a friend of mine who interviewed with them: "If you come to work for us, we'll pay you well. You'll have excellent benefits. And in return, we'll expect you to eat, breathe, sleep, and work for our company. If you work for us, we'll expect our company to come before anything else in your life." They wanted to own him, but he didn't want to be owned by anyone but Christ.

Our compelling purpose in life should be to honor Christ in everything we think, say, and do. If our purpose is to selfishly seek after as much success, pleasure, and approval as we can get, we will pass that selfishness on to our children (in the little time we have left with them).

But if our purpose is to honor Christ, we will use every opportunity to model and teach the character and truth of God to our children. They will be profoundly affected either way!

Changed Affections

The affections of some people have been numbed by years of withdrawal. The affections of others have been replaced by hatred, and their anger has a "hair trigger." Some avoid any intimacy with others because they are afraid of being hurt. Can our fear and sense of distance be overcome? Can anger be changed? Can we choose how we feel?

Well, yes and no. (How's that for a clear answer!) We should not try to change how we feel. If we try to deny or suppress fear or anger, it will only build and, sooner or later, cause either a depression or an explosion. We need to be honest about our emotions and *"pour out our hearts to the Lord."* (Ps. 62:8) We need to ask, *Why am I fearful? Why am I angry? What am I believing about God or about myself that is producing these emotions?* Then we can focus on our thoughts and beliefs, and choose to change what we think about, instead of trying to change how we feel. If we think properly about the Lord and about ourselves, and if these thoughts are modeled to us by an affirming relative or friend, then the emotions will slowly change, too.

And although we cannot change our emotions from negative to positive, we *can* shift them from being destructively negative to being productively negative. Instead of anger, we can experience grief, especially in relation to the disobedience of our children.

The Search For Significance includes this helpful insight:

> *Our sin grieves the Lord; it does not make Him angry.*
> *(Remember, His anger and wrath were averted by Christ's death on the cross.) If we approach our children with an attitude of grief rather than anger when they disobey, it makes a world of difference! What a difference it would make if you approached your children with the attitude and words, "It is sad that you disobeyed. It was harmful to you, and I love you so much that I*

> *don't want you to harm yourself. I will need to discipline you to*
> *help you remember not to do it again. Remember, the reason I am*
> *disciplining you is that I love you so much!"...instead of, "You did*
> *it again, you little brat! I'll make sure you regret it, too!"*
> *(Expletives deleted.)* [2]

Many fathers work fifty-five to sixty hours a week, play golf on Saturday, sleep on Sunday, and are involved in other outside activities. Their schedule doesn't leave much time for their children.

Also, an increasing number of mothers are in the work force. Obviously, some of these are single parents who must work to support their families, but studies show that a large percentage of mothers who work simply want more success, pleasure and approval through their jobs. Their purpose is self-centered. They want more. But what is more important: more possessions or an emotionally healthy family? The acquisition of things takes time and energy that could be devoted to nurturing and developing children.

To change your established schedule so that you have time to be with your children takes courage and planning. As you begin, be sure to plan your time and protect it from the many other demands on you. Don't let anything steal the precious time you have allotted for interaction with the children (and spouse!) God has given you.

Many people have found it meaningful to develop family traditions so that everybody looks forward to the event, and so that, in later years, they can look back on their times together. One father makes chocolate chip pancakes or waffles for his wife and two children every Saturday morning. Another couple takes three hours every Sunday afternoon to spend with their three children. They take the phone off the hook and have a picnic (on the living room floor, if it's raining outside) and read books and play games together.

Traditions can be weekly, monthly, seasonal, or centered around holidays. A list of them is found in the workbook section. Look at these and think of some family traditions that are meaningful to you and your family.

Changed Actions

The first four principles focus on why and when you can model the character of God to your children. This final principle centers on what you model. Good intentions aren't enough. Our children need our time, our attention, our affections, our words, and our deeds.

In their award winning book, *The Blessing*, Gary Smalley and John Trent have examined the way that Isaac blessed his children. We can follow the same example of words and deeds to bless our children. The elements of the blessing are:

- •a meaningful touch
- •a spoken message
- •attaching high value to the one being blessed
- •picturing a special future for the one being blessed, and
- •an active commitment to fulfill the blessing [3]

Touching someone communicates warmth and intimacy. A hug, a pat on the shoulder, or holding a person's hand tells a person that you care, and that you accept and affirm him. A friend of mine, whose family avoided touching each other, determined to give his wife and children meaningful touches each day. He decided to try to touch each one ten times a day until it became a habit for him. Most of us don't have to go to this mechanical extreme, but we would do well to have this same determination.

A spoken message of affection and affirmation is also important. Condemnation and sarcasm are tremendously destructive. It has been estimated that it takes twenty positive messages to overcome every negative one. Some of us have experienced the reverse ratio: twenty negative to one positive! Simple statements have a powerful effect: "I love you." "You're a wonderful son." "You really did that well, honey."

Attaching high value gives another dimension of affirmation. When we communicate that we value a person, it shows him that he has a secure place in our eyes. One friend of mine tells his daughter, "If they lined up all the little girls in the whole world, do you know which one I would pick?"

She always smiles and says, "No, which one, Daddy?"

He waves his finger around like he's in the process of deciding and then points to her and exclaims, "You! You're the one I'd pick!" That's communicating high value.

Picturing a special future involves observing the strengths and abilities of the child. One parent might say, after observing the drawings of his son, "You might become a great artist! You are so good at drawing monsters!" Or to a daughter, "You are so loving and kind, the Lord will use you in hundreds or thousands of people's lives some day!"

Finally, an active commitment to fulfill the blessing is needed. Taking time to observe the children and expending the physical and emotional energy to affirm them are important. Also, we need to provide whatever is necessary to help our children develop and reach the "special future" we have described to them. Baseball practice, piano lessons, crayons and paper, or whatever else we provide for them communicates that we are actively committed to their welfare and development.

As we trust God to change our self-concepts, purposes, affections, schedules, and actions, we will be able to model the character of God to our children, no matter how good or bad that modeling has been for us. There is hope for change! Our children don't have to experience what many of us have.

[1]Charles R. Swindoll, *You and Your Child* (Nashville, TN: Thomas Nelson Publishers, 1977), p.158.
[2]Robert McGee, *The Search For Significance* (Houston, TX: Rapha Publishing, 1987), p. 230.
[3]Gary Smalley and John Trent, *The Blessing* (Nashville, TN: Thomas Nelson Publishers, 1986), p. 24.

Fourteen

BREAKING THE CYCLE:

Responding To Your Parents

This chapter is difficult to write, but it is necessary. It is difficult because responding in a godly way to our parents, especially if they have been abusive or neglectful, can be extremely painful. It is also difficult because each situation is different. Many relationships are complex, and "cookie-cutter" answers don't fit a lot of situations.

But this chapter is necessary because our relationships with our parents are God-given relationships. The Lord wants us to respond to them in a way that honors Him. To do that, we need His wisdom and strength.

Rick and I talked about his relationship with his parents. His father left when Rick was nine years old, and three years later, his parents divorced. His mother had to work to support him and his sister. When she got home each day, she was too tired to give the children much attention and affection. Her affection was sapped, too, by the unresolved bitterness she felt toward her husband.

Rick had received no emotional support from his father and very little from his mother. As we talked about how his family situation had adversely affected his view of God, and how his perception of God could be changed, our conversation eventually came around to how he could respond to his parents now.

Rick's expression became intense. He leaned forward in his chair and said, "It would be easier for me if they were dead!"

I responded carefully, "That may be true, Rick, but they aren't dead, and the Lord can give you the wisdom and strength you need to respond properly to them now."

For some of us, our relationship with our parents has been very good all of our lives, and we need only some minor adjustments in our attitudes and actions toward them. But for others, a major overhaul is in order. Years of withdrawal or bitterness are not overcome in a day, and it takes diligent application of the Word of God as we follow the Spirit of God to enable us to respond properly to our parents.

Some people have been under the domination of their parents to the extent that they feel that they have to say and do exactly what their parents want all the time. Otherwise, they will be criticized and rejected. These people need some objectivity in their relationships with their parents. They need to step away from that domination (without stepping away entirely from their parents) and develop their own identity.

Other people have coped with painful family relationships by going in the other direction. They have withdrawn either emotionally or physically to protect themselves from the pain of parental neglect or disapproval. These people need to pursue their relationships with their parents, extending to them the love and forgiveness of Christ.

In both the Old and New Testaments, the Scriptures direct us to honor our parents:

> *Honor your father and your mother, that your days may be prolonged in the land which the Lord your God gives you.*
> Ex. 20:12

> *Honor your father and mother (which is the first commandment with a promise), that it may be well with you, and that you may live long on the earth.*
> Eph. 6:2-3

But what does it mean to honor our parents? There are many misconceptions about this issue.

People who are very conscientious and overly responsible feel that if their parents aren't completely happy with everything they say and do, then they haven't honored their parents. But the burden of making other people happy is oppressive!

You are not responsible for making your parents happy. That is between them and the Lord. Their contentment and happiness should not rest on your shoulders. They need to depend on the Lord, not you, for their security and significance.

You are *not* responsible for their happiness, but you *are* responsible for developing your own separate identity and then extending your love to them. At that point, you should let them respond in any way they choose to respond. Sometimes, they will appreciate what you say and do. Sometimes, they won't. But you need to do what the Lord wants you to do whether they appreciate it or not.

There is a very helpful statement in *The Search For Significance* that gives objectivity and perspective to honoring our parents. As we develop our own identity and then seek to honor them, we should remember:

> *It would be nice if my father and my mother approve of me, but if they don't, I'm still deeply loved, completely forgiven, fully pleasing, and totally accepted by God.*[1]

Remember, you are not responsible for their happiness, but you are responsible to act in a way that pleases the Lord. Then, let them respond in any way they choose. If they are happy with you, that's fine. If not, be content that you have obeyed and pleased the Lord. After all, He is the Lord, and He deserves our primary affection and obedience. Paul wrote that we can be bond-servants either to people or to the Lord, but not to both.

> *For am I now seeking the favor of men, or of God? Or am I striving to please men? If I were still trying to please men, I would not be a bond-servant of Christ.*
>
> Gal. 1:10

We are responsible to treat our parents in a way that pleases the Lord. Our parents' response is then up to them.

As we develop our own identity and express the Lord's love and grace to our parents, they may well notice a difference in us. But they may not like it! If we have been withdrawn, they may not know how to handle our expressions of gratitude and acts of love. If we have been virtual puppets, doing anything and everything we can to make them happy, our new identities and healthy independence from them is a threat to their domination of us. In that case, even loving actions and words will often be misunderstood because our new independence is seen, in their jaded, self-preoccupied view, as dishonoring to them. Any change in the status quo can be disturbing to our parents, and the transition to a new relationship with them is often awkward.

Many people expect that treating their parents differently will cause their parents to change and treat them differently. That may happen after a while, but then again, it may not. In fact, no matter how much *you* change, they may not change at all! You can pray for their response. You can love them and accept them unconditionally. You can try to do everything perfectly (but, of course, nobody can do that) and they *still* may not change. Don't fall into the trap of feeling that it's up to you to get them to change their opinion of you and their response to you. (That's bargaining. See Chapter Eleven.) They have their own free wills, and they make their own choices. Be content that you are doing all you know to do, learning by trial and error, depending on the Lord for His love and His strength, and let them respond. *They* may never change–but *you* can!

Let's take a look at some principles that will help you respond to your parents in a way that honors the Lord.

See Yourself As a Conqueror, Not a Victim

Some people have experienced extraordinarily tragic family situations. They have been emotionally and physically abused. They have been neglected or abandoned. They have been manipulated to accomplish the selfish goals of their parents. If you haven't come from a family like this, it is hard to comprehend the anguish and trauma that such a family can cause.

But Christ can bring light out of darkness, and purpose out of pain. He can enable us to have hope and confidence because His grace is even bigger than our pain. Because we are His children, we can see ourselves as conquerors instead of victims. Paul wrote to the believers in Rome about this perspective in the midst of his most severe difficulties.

> *Who shall separate us from the love of Christ? Shall tribulation, or distress, or persecution, or famine, or nakedness, or peril, or sword?...But in all these things we overwhelmingly conquer through Him who loved us.*
>
> Rom. 8:35, 37

If we see ourselves as victims, we will always be on the defensive, blaming others for the way we are. But if we see ourselves as conquerors, we will have a deep sense of both purpose and thankfulness, realizing that God uses difficulties to build strength of character in us. And He will use these difficulties to enable us to understand the needs of others so that we can be used as His instruments to help meet those needs.

See Your Parents As People, Not Villains

Young children see their parents as gods. What they say is Truth. What they demand is Law. How they act is the Order of the Universe. Sooner or later, we realize that our parents aren't gods after all, and with that realization comes a conclusion. We either understand that they are more or less ordinary people, or we believe that they are villains who have maliciously hurt us.

The truth is: very few parents intentionally hurt their children. The vast majority are simply living out their own heritage. They treat their children in the same way they have been treated by their own parents. Most of them, far from being evil villains, experience deep pains of guilt and shame because they know they aren't the parents they want to be.

Paula's mother was a kind and gracious lady to most people, but she was a demanding tyrant to Paula. No matter how well Paula performed, it wasn't good enough for her mother, and nothing escaped her jaundiced eye: Paula's grades, her appearance, her friends, her activities; every facet of her life. Paula tried everything to please her mother, but constant disapproval and criticism had caused Paula to become passive and withdrawn.

When she realized that she had been her mother's pawn all of her life, Paula became bitter toward her. After a few months of anger, Paula traveled to visit her mother's parents who lived across the country. She hadn't visited them for a long time, but after only one day, she had a startling revelation. Her grandmother was a harsh and demanding woman. Her mother had never received love and affirmation, only criticism and disapproval. Paula realized that her mother had treated her in the same way that she had been treated!

Instantly, Paula understood that her mother was not the villain that she had thought! She was a person who had been deeply hurt and condemned all her life by *her* mother.

The pain Paula had felt from the constant criticism by her mother remained, but her bitterness turned to grief as she understood that both she and her mother had never experienced the love they needed.

Our parents are not gods, but they usually aren't evil villains either. They are usually people who treat us in the same way they have been treated. Many of them are deeply hurt themselves. They need our understanding, not our condemnation.

Develop a Healthy Sense of Independence

Some people base their whole identity on their parents. This is understandable for a child, but it is devastating for an adult. As people mature, they need to develop their own identity.

Helen's father seemed to have a split personality. Most of the time, he was quiet and unassuming, even passive. But on occasion, he would explode in a profane fury. Helen was deeply scarred by her father's mixed signals. She was fearful and insecure.

Her fear and insecurity didn't change as she grew older. She married and had children, but she cowered at the slightest change in her husband's tone of voice. She needed help.

When I asked her about her father, she could describe his behavior very accurately. But when I asked how she had felt when he was in a rage, she couldn't respond. "I...I'm not sure how I felt," she stammered.

"Did you feel afraid of him?"

"I don't know."

We were obviously getting no where fast, so I decided to be more objective. "Helen," I asked, "how would you feel if you saw a man in your neighborhood treat his daughter the way you were treated?"

"I'd be angry," she responded.

"Would you?"

"Yes, I'd be really angry with him!" Now there was intensity in her eyes and voice.

"How would a normal, little girl feel about a father like yours?"

"Well, I guess she'd be afraid of him. I guess she'd be very hurt and afraid." The lights began to come on in Helen's mind. "I guess I'm just numb about my father."

Most of us have a difficult time being objective about our parents. The feelings–and the defense mechanisms to block the pain–are so strong that we have a hard time establishing an identity that is separate from their opinions of us. But we must have a healthy sense of distance from our parents if we are to both live fully for Christ and respond properly to them.

I advised Helen to think of her father as "that man in the neighborhood" for a while, until she could look at him and at herself more objectively. She allowed herself to feel normal emotions of hurt and anger as she thought about how she would feel if she saw him enraged at his daughter for no good reason. Soon she was able to transfer those objective perceptions to her own father.

Helen was progressively able to develop a healthy independence from him. She was able to begin to develop a separate identity based on the truths of God's Word, instead of the unreasoned fury of an unbalanced father. It was a long process, but it is making a world of difference to Helen and her family.

Make Godly Choices

The goal of our lives is to bring honor to the Lord. Consequently, the goal of our every activity and relationship is to honor Him. If a person has been deeply hurt by his or her parents, the normal response is either withdrawal to avoid pain or revenge to inflict pain (or some combination of these). But withdrawal and revenge do not honor Christ.

As a person begins to understand, believe, and live by the truths of Christ's unconditional love and acceptance, he is then able to begin expressing that love and acceptance to others. In fact, it can be said that a person is able to *express* God's love, forgiveness, and acceptance only in proportion to his *experience* of it himself. Therefore, we need to drink deeply of these powerful truths so that our relationships can be characterized by them. Paul and John flatly stated that our ability to love, forgive, and accept others is based on our own experience:

> *The Samaritan woman therefore said to Him, "How is it that You, being a Jew, ask me for a drink since I am a Samaritan woman?" (For Jews have no dealings with Samaritans.) Jesus answered and said to her, "If you knew the gift of God, and who it is who says to you, 'Give Me a drink,' you would have asked Him, and He would have given you living water." She said to Him, "Sir, You have nothing to draw with and the well is deep; where then do You get that living water?"*
>
> John 4:9-11

> *...bearing with one another, and forgiving each other, whoever has a complaint against anyone; just as the Lord forgave you, so also should you.* Col. 3:13

> *Wherefore, accept one another, just as Christ also accepted us to the glory of God.* Rom. 15:7

Until we begin developing our new identity in Christ, we have no choice but to simply try to defend ourselves as best we can, and withdraw from or punish those who have hurt us. But, when we realize that Christ is our Protector, and that He is the complete source of our security and significance, then we can choose to act in a way that is best for others and honoring to Him. We can take our attention off of ourselves, and put it on Christ and others because we are secure.

Sounds good, doesn't it? It is good, but the transition from self-defense and revenge, to unconditional acceptance of others who have deeply hurt us is awkward, long, and difficult. Our emotions often go haywire. When our emotions tell us to fight back or hide and the Scriptures tell us to believe the truth about ourselves and love others, we need to have the courage to live by the truth instead of our emotions. Many of us have been living by our emotions all of our lives, so the new choice to live by truth—in spite of our painful emotions—is difficult, indeed. But seeing our emotions objectively and knowing that they are often based on our old identity is at least half of the battle.

The transition may be difficult, and you may need a friend's advice and encouragement to keep going in the midst of the battle. But our lives are a series of choices: will we choose to live by withdrawal and revenge, or by the truth of the Scriptures and the power of God's Spirit?

Some people realize, after their parents have died, that they can choose to love, forgive, and accept their parents. But it's too late. Then, the potential for a reconciliation with their parents is gone. This can be very disappointing, but instead of letting this disappointment lead to bitterness, they can realize that God is sovereign. He is aware of the situation, and He doesn't demand anything that is beyond reason. Those whose parents have already died can thank God for what they have learned about His character, and share their newfound wisdom with those whose parents are still living. Then another family will have the potential for reconciliation.

Be Prepared

It may sound spiritual to believe that if you change, then your parents will automatically change overnight. However, it took years (generations) for your family to develop behavior patterns, and it will probably take more than one conversation to rectify all its wrongs and develop new habits of relating. It may even take years for you to change. And they may never change.

Be prepared for your communications with your parents. Don't expect them to change very quickly. They may. But they may not. They may even think that you are attacking them, and your desire for reconciliation may at first produce more bitterness.

Darren was from an alcoholic family. His father was neglectful and abusive. His mother was a perfectionist. Darren began to understand how he had been affected by his parents and, on one occasion, he asked, "What should I tell my parents about what I'm learning?"

I asked, "What would happen if you told them?"

He answered, "They would be furious!"

"Then tell them only what would be positive and helpful to them and to your relationship with them."

Darren changed his game plan from bluntly telling everything to his parents to carefully planning his communication with them.

Fortify yourself with the truth so that when you talk with them, you can remember that you are deeply loved, completely forgiven, fully pleasing, and totally accepted by the Lord, no matter what they (or anyone else) think of you. Then you can make the choice to love them, whatever their response might be. Then you can make the hard but right choices, even though your emotions tell you to withdraw or attack.

Responding to parents can be very difficult. Don't be naive about the difficulties. Ask God for His wisdom and power, and be prepared.

[1]Robert McGee, *The Search For Significance* (Houston, TX: Rapha Publishing, 1987), p. 225.

THE
PARENT FACTOR

WORKBOOK SECTION

Introduction

How To Use
This Workbook

This workbook is divided into steps. Follow the directions given for each one. Here are some general suggestions:

1. Review chapters in the book

Take time to review corresponding chapters of the book as you go through the steps; the chapters will offer fresh meaning as you work through them.

2. Write out your responses

It's really important for you to use a pen or pencil with the workbook and actually complete the tasks assigned. If you have a habit of *mentally* answering questions on inventories instead of writing out the answers, *break your habit!* Studies show that you will profit five to eight times more if you write out your responses.

3. Follow each step's time frame

Some of the steps only require a few minutes of your time to complete. Others are designed to be done over a number of days. All are designed to cause you to expand your awareness of the character of God.

4. Don't rush through the material

When you receive a new insight, stop to think and pray. Meditate on what you are learning. The goal is not to get through the material as quickly as you can. The goal is to understand and apply what you learn. It is more important that you take the time to reflect and absorb the content than it is for you to keep up some arbitrary pace.

Note: Steps 1-5 provide various ways to analyze how your family has shaped your view of God and affected your life. These steps cover more or less the same ground in different ways. Though these steps may seem redundant to some people, most of us have a great need for objectivity. These steps, then, can provide more insight and perception by looking at the same issues from a variety of angles.

EVALUATING YOUR RELATIONSHIP
WITH YOUR FATHER

On the next page, there is an exercise to help you evaluate your relationship between you and your father as you were growing up. Check the appropriate square as you recall how he related to you when you were young. Here's an example:

EXAMPLE:

Characteristics	Always	Very Often	Some-times	Hardly Ever	Never	Don't Know
Gentle			✓			
Stern	✓					
Loving			✓			
Aloof			✓			
Disapproving		✓				
Distant	✓					

WHEN I WAS A CHILD, MY FATHER WAS...

Characteristics	Always	Very Often	Some-times	Hardly Ever	Never	Don't Know
Gentle						
Stern						
Loving						
Aloof						
Disapproving						
Distant						
Close and Intimate						
Kind						
Angry						
Caring						
Demanding						
Supportive						
Interested						
Discipliner						
Gracious						
Harsh						
Wise						
Holy						
Leader						
Provider						
Trustworthy						
Joyful						
Forgiving						
Good						
Cherishing of Me						
Compassionate						
Impatient						
Unreasonable						
Strong						
Protective						
Passive						
Encouraging						
Sensitive						
Just						
Unpredictable						

EVALUATION OF YOUR RELATIONSHIP
WITH YOUR FATHER:

1. What does this inventory tell you about your relationship with your father?

_____

_____

_____

_____

_____

_____

_____

_____

_____

2. If you were an objective observer of the type of relationship you have just described, how would you feel about the father?

_____

_____

_____

_____

_____

_____

_____

_____

_____

3. About the child?

_____
_____
_____
_____
_____
_____
_____
_____
_____
_____

4. How would you respond to the father? Be specific.

_____
_____
_____
_____
_____
_____
_____
_____
_____
_____

5. To the child?

_____
_____
_____
_____
_____
_____
_____
_____

EVALUATING YOUR RELATIONSHIP
WITH YOUR MOTHER

On the next page, there is an exercise to help you evaluate your relationship between you and your mother as you were growing up. Check the appropriate square as you recall how she related to you when you were young. Here's an example:

EXAMPLE:

Characteristics	Always	Very Often	Some-times	Hardly Ever	Never	Don't Know
Gentle			✓			
Stern	✓					
Loving			✓			
Aloof			✓			
Disapproving		✓				
Distant	✓					

WHEN I WAS A CHILD, MY MOTHER WAS...

Characteristics	Always	Very Often	Some-times	Hardly Ever	Never	Don't Know
Gentle						
Stern						
Loving						
Aloof						
Disapproving						
Distant						
Close and Intimate						
Kind						
Angry						
Caring						
Demanding						
Supportive						
Interested						
Discipliner						
Gracious						
Harsh						
Wise						
Holy						
Leader						
Provider						
Trustworthy						
Joyful						
Forgiving						
Good						
Cherishing of Me						
Compassionate						
Impatient						
Unreasonable						
Strong						
Protective						
Passive						
Encouraging						
Sensitive						
Just						
Unpredictable						

EVALUATION OF YOUR RELATIONSHIP
WITH YOUR MOTHER:

1. What does this inventory tell you about your relationship with your mother?

_____

_____

_____

_____

_____

_____

_____

_____

_____

_____

2. If you were an objective observer of the type of relationship you have just described, how would you feel about the mother?

_____

_____

_____

_____

_____

_____

_____

_____

_____

3. About the child?

_____
_____
_____
_____
_____
_____
_____
_____
_____
_____

4. How would you respond to the mother? Be specific.

_____
_____
_____
_____
_____
_____
_____
_____
_____
_____

5. To the child?

_____
_____
_____
_____
_____
_____
_____

EVALUATING YOUR
RELATIONSHIP WITH GOD

This inventory is designed to help you evaluate your relationship with God. Because it is subjective, there are no right or wrong answers. To ensure that the test reveals your actual feelings, please follow the instructions carefully.

1. Answer openly and honestly. Don't respond from a theological knowledge of God, but from personal experience.

2. Don't describe what the relationship *ought to be*, or what you hope it *will be*, but what it *is* right now.

3. Some people feel God might be displeased if they give a negative answer. Nothing is further from the truth. He is pleased with our honesty. A foundation of transparency is required for growth to occur.

4. Turn each characteristic into a question. For example: *To what degree do I really feel God loves me? To what degree do I really feel that God understands me?*

5. Recall times of stress and difficulty, as well as normal situations, as you respond.

TO WHAT DEGREE DO I REALLY FEEL GOD IS...

Characteristics	Always	Very Often	Some-times	Hardly Ever	Never	Don't Know
Gentle						
Stern						
Loving						
Aloof						
Disapproving						
Distant						
Close and Intimate						
Kind						
Angry						
Caring						
Demanding						
Supportive						
Interested						
Discipliner						
Gracious						
Harsh						
Wise						
Holy						
Leader						
Provider						
Trustworthy						
Joyful						
Forgiving						
Good						
Cherishing of Me						
Compassionate						
Impatient						
Unreasonable						
Strong						
Protective						
Passive						
Encouraging						
Sensitive						
Just						
Unpredictable						

1. What does this exercise tell you about your relationship with God?

_____

_____

_____

_____

_____

_____

_____

_____

2. Are there any differences between what you know (theologically) and how you feel (emotionally) about Him? If so, what are they?

_____

_____

_____

_____

_____

_____

_____

_____

YOUR FATHER'S INFLUENCE
AND YOUR PERCEPTION OF GOD

How has your relationship with your father influenced your perception of your Heavenly Father? To get a comparison, transfer all the check marks you made for your father on page 144 to the *shaded columns* on page 156. Use a check mark for this category.

When you have completed this, transfer the check marks you made on page 152 which relate to your relationship with God. To make them more obvious, use an "**✗**" for this category. Put them in the *white columns* in the appropriate places.

EXAMPLE:

Characteristics	Always	Very Often	Some-times	Hardly Ever	Never	Don't Know
Gentle		✗	✓			
Stern	✓	✗				
Loving		✗	✓			
Aloof	✓			✗		
Disapproving			✓			

Instructions: Transfer all check marks from page 144 to the SHADED columns. Transfer all check marks from page 152 to the WHITE columns.

Characteristics	Always	Very Often	Some-times	Hardly Ever	Never	Don't Know
Gentle						
Stern						
Loving						
Aloof						
Disapproving						
Distant						
Close and Intimate						
Kind						
Angry						
Caring						
Demanding						
Supportive						
Interested						
Discipliner						
Gracious						
Harsh						
Wise						
Holy						
Leader						
Provider						
Trustworthy						
Joyful						
Forgiving						
Good						
Cherishing of Me						
Compassionate						
Impatient						
Unreasonable						
Strong						
Protective						
Passive						
Encouraging						
Sensitive						
Just						
Unpredictable						

What Did You Learn?

1. Which characteristics are the same for both your father and your Heavenly Father?

_____

_____

_____

_____

_____

_____

_____

2. Which characteristics are quite different (two or more boxes away from each other)?

_____

_____

_____

_____

_____

_____

_____

3. What patterns (if any) do you see?

_____

_____

_____

_____

_____

_____

_____

4. Write a summary paragraph about how your perception of God has been shaped by your relationship with your father.

_____

_____

_____

_____

_____

_____

_____

_____

_____

_____

_____

_____

_____

_____

_____

_____

_____

_____

YOUR MOTHER'S INFLUENCE
AND YOUR PERCEPTION OF GOD

How has your mother influenced your perception of your Heavenly Father? To get a comparison, transfer all the check marks you made for your mother on page 148 to the *shaded columns* on page 160. Use a check mark for this category.

When you have completed this, transfer the check marks you made on page 152 which relate to your relationship with God. To make them more obvious, use an "✗" for this category. Put them in the *white columns* in the appropriate places.

EXAMPLE:

Characteristics	Always	Very Often	Some-times	Hardly Ever	Never	Don't Know
Gentle		✗	✔			
Stern	✔	✗				
Loving		✗	✔			
Aloof		✔		✗		
Disapproving			✔			

Instructions: Transfer all check marks from page 148 to the SHADED columns. Transfer all check marks from page 152 to the WHITE columns.

Characteristics	Always	Very Often	Some- times	Hardly Ever	Never	Don't Know
Gentle						
Stern						
Loving						
Aloof						
Disapproving						
Distant						
Close and Intimate						
Kind						
Angry						
Caring						
Demanding						
Supportive						
Interested						
Discipliner						
Gracious						
Harsh						
Wise						
Holy						
Leader						
Provider						
Trustworthy						
Joyful						
Forgiving						
Good						
Cherishing of Me						
Compassionate						
Impatient						
Unreasonable						
Strong						
Protective						
Passive						
Encouraging						
Sensitive						
Just						
Unpredictable						

What Did You Learn?

1. Which characteristics are the same for both your mother and your Heavenly Father?

_____

_____

_____

_____

_____

_____

_____

2. Which characteristics are quite different (two or more boxes away from each other)?

_____

_____

_____

_____

_____

_____

_____

_____

3. What patterns (if any) do you see?

_____

_____

_____

_____

_____

_____

_____

4. Write a summary paragraph about how your perception of God has been shaped by your relationship with your mother.

_____

_____

_____

_____

_____

_____

_____

_____

_____

_____

_____

_____

_____

_____

_____

_____

_____

STEP FOUR

ANALYZING YOUR FAMILY

This exercise will help you remember what the relationships in your family were like as you were growing up. The analysis will help you understand the dynamics of your family relationships and how you have been affected by them.

Check the appropriate box or write your responses to the questions:

1. How would you describe your parent's marriage?
    ❑ Unhappy
    ❑ Poor
    ❑ Good
    ❑ Happy

2. Would you describe your home life as...
    ❑ Unhappy
    ❑ Poor
    ❑ Good
    ❑ Happy

3. Would you describe your father as:

❑ Passive	❑ Gregarious	❑ Angry	❑ Sad	❑ Other
❑ Strong	❑ Gentle	❑ Harsh	❑ Loving	❑ Manipulative

4. Did your father take time to play with you and your brothers and/or sisters?
    ❑ Yes ❑ No

5. Was your father...Dictatorial_____ Indifferent_____
    Interested in you_____ Open_____ Tender_____ Protective_____

6. How important was TV to your father?
    ❑ Addicted to it   ❑ Occasional viewer   ❑ Seldom/Never watched

7. Are you afraid of becoming like your father?   ❑ Yes   ❑ No
    Explain:

    _____
    _____
    _____

8. Would you describe your mother as:
    ❑ Passive   ❑ Gregarious   ❑ Angry   ❑ Sad   ❑ Other
    ❑ Strong   ❑ Gentle   ❑ Harsh   ❑ Loving   ❑ Manipulative

9. Did your mother take time to play with you and your brothers and/or sisters?
    ❑ Yes ❑ No

10. Was your mother...Dictatorial_____ Indifferent_____
    Interested in you_____ Open_____ Tender_____ Protective_____

11. How important was TV to your mother?
❑ Addicted to it   ❑ Occasional viewer   ❑ Seldom/Never watched

12. Are you afraid of becoming like your mother? ❑ Yes   ❑ No
Explain:

_____

_____

_____

_____

_____

13. What did you enjoy doing the most as a child in a family setting?

_____

_____

_____

_____

14. Did your father and mother argue...
❑ Frequently   ❑ Seldom   ❑ Never

15. *a*) Would you classify your parent's economic status as...
❑ upper class   ❑ middle class   ❑ lower class

b) What impact did this economic status have on you?

_____

_____

_____

16. Are your parents living now?
    Mother:
    ❑ Yes   ❑ No

    Father:
    ❑ Yes   ❑ No

17. *a)* Describe your relationship with your father:

    _____
    _____
    _____
    _____
    _____
    _____

    b) ...with your mother:

    _____
    _____
    _____
    _____
    _____

18. *a)* Did your father demonstrate affection toward your mother?
    ❑ Yes   ❑ No

    If so, how? If not, why not?

    _____
    _____
    _____
    _____
    _____

b) Did your mother demonstrate affection toward your father?

❏ Yes   ❏ No

If so, how? If not, why not?

_____

_____

_____

_____

_____

19. Are you close to your brothers and sisters?

❏ Yes   ❏ No

Explain:

_____

_____

_____

_____

_____

20. *a*) Were you teased as a child?

❏ Yes   ❏ No

b) If "yes", what about?

_____

_____

_____

c) Who teased you the most?

_____

_____

_____

_____

d) What was your emotional response?

_____

_____

_____

_____

21. *a*) Were you ever sexually fondled as a child by any member of your family?
❑ Yes   ❑ No

b) By someone else?
❑ Yes   ❑ No

22. *a*) Did you try to manipulate your parents to get attention or special treatment?
❑ Yes   ❑ No

b) If so, how?

_____

_____

_____

_____

_____

23. *a*) Did your parents agree with each other on how to discipline you?
❑ Yes   ❑ No

b) Describe how you were disciplined when you were a child:

_____

_____

_____

24. *a*) Did you ever have any serious illness as a child?
❏ Yes ❏ No

b) If so, how did this affect you and your relationship with your parents and siblings?

_____

_____

_____

25. Was there anything about you for which your parents communicated consistent disapproval? If so, what?

_____

_____

_____

26. *a*) Are there any periods of your life you cannot remember?
❏ Yes ❏ No

b) If so, which period(s)?

_____

_____

_____

_____

_____

_____

27. Which parent did you enjoy being with the most as a child?
❏ Father ❏ Mother

Why?

_____

_____

28. Has this exercise prompted any feelings in you about your home life? If so, describe them:

_____

_____

_____

_____

_____

_____

Observations and Analysis

Imagine that you are a consultant in family relationships. You have just reviewed the answers written in Step Four, and you are asked to give an impartial analysis to your professional colleagues about this family. Write out your conclusions:

1. What are the strengths of this family?

_____

_____

_____

_____

_____

_____

2. What are some of the difficulties of this family?

_____

_____

_____

_____

_____

3. Describe the relationship of the husband and wife:

_____

_____

_____

_____

_____

_____

_____

_____

4. Describe the father's relationship with each child:

_____

_____

_____

_____

_____

_____

5. Describe the mother's relationship with each child:

_____

_____

_____

_____

_____

_____

6. How was the character of God modeled by these parents?

_____

_____

_____

_____

_____

_____

7.　How was the character of God distorted by these parents?

_____

_____

_____

_____

_____

Introduction

Steps Five, Six, And Seven

Step Five: Analyzing Symptoms

In Step Five, you will be like a doctor in an examination room. The first thing a physician does with a patient is consider his symptoms. Next, he seeks to locate the cause of those symptoms and, finally, he prescribes the remedy.

F. Delitzsch writes, "As children receive their nature from their parents...so they have also to bear and atone for their fathers' guilt." History does repeat itself. Either we learn from it, or we are doomed to repeat it. Time and again, couples recycle their family life in patterns that are almost identical to what they experienced as children. Without intending to, they "pass the sins of the fathers on to the third and fourth generations." (Ex. 34:7)

The following will give you an opportunity to analyze your parents from several different angles. Although further analysis of your family may, at this point, seem redundant, many of us lack objectivity about our families. This exercise will enable some to gain new insights about their parents as a result of looking at the same issues form a variety of different ways.

Steps Six and Seven: God's Remedies

God can intervene and interrupt the passing of problems from one generation to the next. He can bring healing and stability and grace to fractured families and hurting people. He alone can make it possible for us to focus on the future instead of the past.

EXAMINING

CHARACTERISTICS

One of the basic principles of spiritual growth is that it is difficult to understand present situations apart from a knowledge of the past. As you examine characteristics of your parents' lives, you can reflect on the impact they have had on your life as well.

Two sections follow. Section I will help you identify characteristics in your father. Section II will help you identify characteristics in your mother.

These characteristics have been compiled from scores of cases. Of necessity, they are broad and general, and some may seem to overlap with others.

HOW TO CONDUCT THE EXAMINATION

Remember that each characteristic is meant to examine your father's and mother's lives, not yours. Each symptom is described by its title. For example, one of them is listed as:

Your Father's Parents: Dominant Mother/Passive Father

Each title is followed by a brief explanation of the characteristic. For example, the one above is explained in this way:

In this home, the mother is dominant (in effect, if not in personality), while the father is passive. When a son from such a home marries, it is often to a girl with the same degree of female domination he experienced from his mother. History then repeats itself.

Indicate on a scale of 0 (not evident at all) to 10 (definitely evident) the extent the trait is present in your parent.

Example:

Indicate the degree to which your father had a dominant mother and a passive father in his childihood:

CHARACTERISTICS
OF YOUR FATHER

Indicate on a scale of 0 (not evident at all) to 10 (definitely evident) the extent to which the following traits are present in your father:

Your Father's Parents: Dominant Mother/Passive Father

In this home, the mother is dominant (in effect, if not in personality), while the father is passive. When a son from such a home marries, it is often to a girl with the same degree of female domination he experienced from his mother. History then repeats itself.

```
0   1   2   3   4   5   6   7   8   9   10
└───┴───┴───┴───┴───┴───┴───┴───┴───┴───┘
```

Your Father's Mother: Maternal Hostility or Dependence

If your father has developed hostility toward his mother over the years, that hostility is often transferred to his wife. The same is true of dependence. If he has been overly dependent on his mother, he may be the same way with his wife.

```
0   1   2   3   4   5   6   7   8   9   10
└───┴───┴───┴───┴───┴───┴───┴───┴───┴───┘
```

Your Father's Anger Toward His Father

In your father, there may be a deep desire for a relationship with his father which was not provided in his boyhood years. If this relationship wasn't strong and intimate, there is often a deep-rooted hostility toward his father, making it hard to have a strong and intimate relationship with his own children.

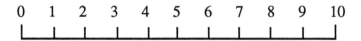

0   1   2   3   4   5   6   7   8   9   10

Your Father's Emotional Immaturity

As a husband he wants to be babied. He has not matured to become an adult role model for his own children. He might even *resent* his children and be jealous of the attention they receive from his wife.

0   1   2   3   4   5   6   7   8   9   10

Your Father's Emotional Instability

Your father's emotional makeup is quite fragile when compared to the emotional strength of your mother. The children see her, not him, as the strength of the home.

0   1   2   3   4   5   6   7   8   9   10

Your Father's Insecurity in Relationships

Your father tends to be quite insecure in interpersonal relationships in the home. He is unable to give himself deeply to his wife or children.

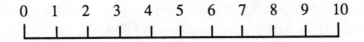

Your Father's Poor Self-Image

Your father is not confident of his own abilities. He often belittles himself as one who is inadequate and incapable.

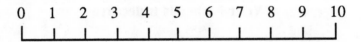

Your Father's Sense of Inadequacy

The fear of failure can be overpowering in his own mind. It keeps him from reaching his full potential. Sometimes it keeps him locked into jobs that are beneath his true capacities.

Your Father's Feelings of Insignificance

Feeling insignificant can cause withdrawal on the one hand, or a pugnacious attitude on the other. He feels inferior to his wife, especially in group settings.

Your Father Feels Parental and Spouse Disapproval

Your father feels that nothing he does is good enough for his parents and his wife. He is the object of sarcasm and disgust.

0   1   2   3   4   5   6   7   8   9   10
|____|____|____|____|____|____|____|____|____|____|

Your Father Displays a Maternal Affection Drive

If your father has grown up in an "absent-mother" home, or has been doted upon by a possessive mother, he may show a strong desire for maternal affection from his wife, expecting her to "mother" him.

0   1   2   3   4   5   6   7   8   9   10
|____|____|____|____|____|____|____|____|____|____|

Your Father Is Indecisive

Your father avoids making decisions, especially in family situations. He leaves the decision-making to your mother. Then he can blame her when things go wrong.

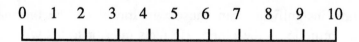

0   1   2   3   4   5   6   7   8   9   10
|____|____|____|____|____|____|____|____|____|____|

Your Father Is Stoic

Your father tends to be non-expressive. He does not relate

emotionally to others in the home. He represses, rather than expresses, his emotions, though his emotions may explode from time to time.

```
0   1   2   3   4   5   6   7   8   9   10
└───┴───┴───┴───┴───┴───┴───┴───┴───┴───┘
```

Your Father Is Non-Communicative

He avoids intense discussions, especially those of a personal nature. He refuses to communicate if he feels he is being attacked. He expects his wife to *know* what he is thinking.

```
0   1   2   3   4   5   6   7   8   9   10
└───┴───┴───┴───┴───┴───┴───┴───┴───┴───┘
```

Your Father Is a Perfectionist

His legacy from childhood is a poor self-image. As a result, he has overstructured his world. It's his way of controlling it. He lives by a self-imposed set of rules and ritually obeys them. He makes similar demands on his wife and children to "keep the rules." Yet, he never seems to be pleased with the results, no matter how well his rules are kept.

```
0   1   2   3   4   5   6   7   8   9   10
└───┴───┴───┴───┴───┴───┴───┴───┴───┴───┘
```

Your Father Is Domineering

His sense of inadequacy is often shown in a tyrannical attitude toward his wife and children.

```
0   1   2   3   4   5   6   7   8   9   10
└───┴───┴───┴───┴───┴───┴───┴───┴───┴───┘
```

Your Father Is Sarcastic

He tends to put down his wife in public, humiliating her before her friends. He also belittles her privately, and is unable to compliment her on her strengths.

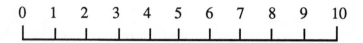

Your Father Twists Things Around

He often twists what his wife says or does, creating the illusion that she is always wrong, while he is always right.

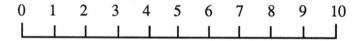

Your Father Is a Workaholic

He gains his identity through his work; so, he is driven to work long, hard hours to be a success.

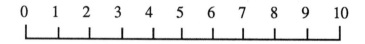

Your Father Has a Weak Character

He tends to be weak in character strength, especially in relation to his wife. He lets her dominate him.

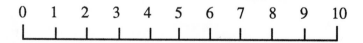

Your Father Is Self-Centered

He is selfish, demanding that his wife and children stop whatever they are doing to wait on him. He truly believes his own needs are so important that other activities being performed by family members should be dropped at his request.

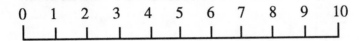

Your Father Is Aroused Easily

He will demand sex whenever he wants it. He uses sex as his "security blanket."

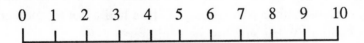

Your Father Has a Childish Attitude

He tends to portray a "little boy" attitude toward his wife, who says, "My husband is more of a child than my children."

0   1   2   3   4   5   6   7   8   9   10

Your Father Has an "Ostrich" Syndrome

He tends to avoid controversy and conflict. He "buries his head in the sand" hoping problems will go away.

0   1   2   3   4   5   6   7   8   9   10

Your Father Is Self-Righteous

He tends to pull the cloak of religion about him when his wife attacks him or becomes disgusted with him.

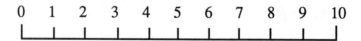

Your Father Tries to Maintain the Status Quo

He resists seeking outside help in marital problems. He relates getting counseling to an admission of personal failure. His tendency is to avoid "rocking the boat," hoping that the problems will work themselves out, or that they aren't as bad as his wife says they are.

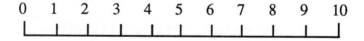

Your Father Tries to Be a Father to His Wife

Being a good father is his strongest point, but it can affect his marriage adversely if he also tries to be a father to his wife. If he is from a home where his mother was absent, or if he had a doting mother, he may display a sibling rivalry with his own children.

```
0   1   2   3   4   5   6   7   8   9   10
L___I___I___I___I___I___I___I___I___I___J
```

Your Father Abdicates Leadership

He resists taking a leadership role in the home or with his children, forcing his wife into the dominant role. This type of person can be, and often is, a very strong leader outside the home.

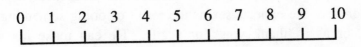

Your Father Attempts to Buy Affection

He tries to prove himself to his wife and children, gaining their approval and getting strokes by giving them *things* rather than *himself*.

0   1   2   3   4   5   6   7   8   9   10

Your Father Is Prone Toward Failure

His self-esteem is so low that he seems to set himself up for failure. He won't really try to succeed, because if he really tried and still failed, the pain would be too great. So he reasons, *If I don't try very hard, then failure isn't so disgraceful.*

0   1   2   3   4   5   6   7   8   9   10

Your Father Has Homosexual Feelings

He has latent needs to be loved and affirmed by his father, causing great inner turmoil. Sometimes this man is an active homosexual, even if he is married.

0   1   2   3   4   5   6   7   8   9   10

Your Father Is a Manipulator

He manipulates people to get what he wants from them, especially in the area of sex. He expects sex as the result of doing something nice for his wife, or as a "thank you" for a gift. He can make his wife feel prostituted.

```
0   1   2   3   4   5   6   7   8   9   10
```

Your Father Relates Better to Women Than Men

It is far easier for him to open up to a woman than to a man. He tends to be quiet and withdrawn around men.

```
0   1   2   3   4   5   6   7   8   9   10
```

Your Father Is Intimidated

He is intimidated by his wife's abilities, success, and popularity. He is also intimidated by older men or men of status.

```
0   1   2   3   4   5   6   7   8   9   10
```

Your Father Doubts His Masculinity

He tends to doubt his masculinity and worries about his height, athletic abilities, amount of hair on his chest, etc.

```
0   1   2   3   4   5   6   7   8   9   10
```

Your Father Is Possessive

He tends to be possessive and fearful, afraid of any attention given to his wife by others.

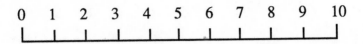

0   1   2   3   4   5   6   7   8   9   10

Your Father Is Demanding

He is spoiled. He wants his way.

0   1   2   3   4   5   6   7   8   9   10

Your Father Is Unforgiving

He says he forgives his family's mistakes and sins, but by bringing them up again and again, he shows he hasn't forgiven them at all.

0   1   2   3   4   5   6   7   8   9   10

Your Father Has a "Victim Mentality"

He feels he is the victim of being misunderstood and abused, and he always points out that he is not guilty. He often feels that he has been sinned against.

0   1   2   3   4   5   6   7   8   9   10

Your Father and Mother Parent Each Other

His marriage is a relationship in which he plays "daddy" to his wife, while she "mothers" him in return.

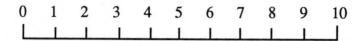

Your Father Has Problems of Omission

His problems are often the result of what he does *not* do, rather than the result of doing wrong things. He does not get drunk, for example, but his omission of love and tenderness for his family has been just as devastating.

```
0   1   2   3   4   5   6   7   8   9   10
```

Your Father Has a Poor "Father God" Concept

His concept of God is usually faulty. He finds it impossible to relate to God in a personal prayer life. He may go through the motions religiously, but he has abdicated as the spiritual leader of his family.

```
0   1   2   3   4   5   6   7   8   9   10
```

Your Father Distrusts His Wife

He particularly distrusts his wife's relationships with other men. This severely limits her freedom to the point that she is even afraid to speak to another man.

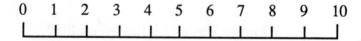

Your Father Is a Show Off

He tends to "show off" his wife, as a father would his daughter. Or, he may embarrass his wife by discussing her bodily features in front of other men. Or, he may be a "name dropper," seeking to impress others by his contact with famous persons.

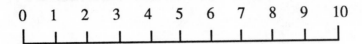

Your Father Is Self-Sufficient

He tries to perform, through his own efforts, things which only God can do through His efforts. He calls attention to his accomplishments with no thought of giving glory to God.

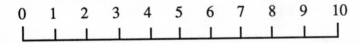

Your Father Is Conscientious Outside the Home

He is often quite responsible outside of the home, even when he takes no responsibility for what happens to the people in his own family.

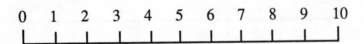

Your Father Is Meticulous

He can be meticulous to the point of distraction. Everybody in the family is frustrated by his "nit-picking."

0   1   2   3   4   5   6   7   8   9   10

Your Father Is Inflexible

His sense of inadequacy and fear of failure can make him quite inflexible.

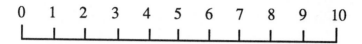

Your Father Is Competitive

He vicariously competes through his children, or he competes directly with other men in business, sports, or conversation.

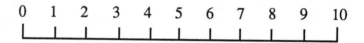

Your Father Is Flirty

He often flirts with women. He is very attracted to young women, and feels more comfortable with them than with men.

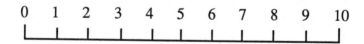

Your Father Is Isolated

He keeps to himself, isolating his feelings from others.

Your Father Is Defensive

He is defensive when questioned about anything he has said or done.

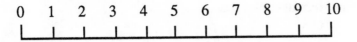

Your Father Is Too Busy

He can be quite self-possessed and rigid in the use of his time. He can stay so busy that he shuts out others from being close to him.

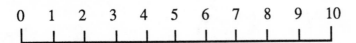

Your Father Cannot Distinguish Clearly Between a Wife and Mother

He treats his wife more like a mother than a wife. Sexual intimacy may be infrequent because of this.

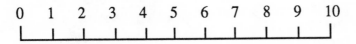

Your Father Is Non-Assertive

He is particularly non-assertive in the home, and often is the same way on the job.

Your Father Is Sensitive

He reacts negatively to criticism or supposed slights. He gets his feelings hurt over things that should not matter. He can become abusive to those around him at such times.

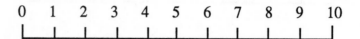

Your Father Lacks Ambition

He hides laziness behind a religious facade if he is a Christian, and will rationalize his laziness if he is not a believer. He may go without employment for long periods of time.

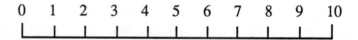

How Have These Symptoms Affected You?

Go back through each of your responses in this section and answer the following questions:

1. Which traits concerning your *father* were most evident (seven or more on the scale)? List these:

_____

_____

_____

_____

_____

_____

_____

_____

_____

_____

2. How have each of these affected you? Be specific.

_____

_____

_____

_____

_____

_____

_____

_____

_____

_____

3. Do you see any of these traits (those you listed in questions 1 and 2) in your life, your marriage, or your relationship with your children? If so, which ones?

_____

_____

_____

_____

_____

_____

_____

_____

_____

_____

_____

CHARACTERISTICS
OF YOUR MOTHER

Indicate on a scale of 0 (not evident at all) to 10 (definitely evident) the extent to which each of these traits were (are) present in your mother:

Your Mother's Parents: Dominant Mother/Passive Father

Your mother's mother was dominant in her family and her father was passive. Therefore, she has ambivalent feelings toward her father (a love-hate relationship), but tends to be critical of her mother. She has a fear of becoming like her mother.

```
0   1   2   3   4   5   6   7   8   9   10
|___|___|___|___|___|___|___|___|___|___|
```

Your Mother Is Attracted to Other Men

She tends to be attracted to passive males. Passive men seem to be "safe," but this passivity becomes a problem to her after her marriage. She may have married a man much like her own passive father. She may have an affair with a man who has characteristics similar to her husband. If she divorces her husband, she will probably marry a man with similar passive characteristics.

```
0   1   2   3   4   5   6   7   8   9   10
|___|___|___|___|___|___|___|___|___|___|
```

Your Mother Has a Transference of Hostility

Hostility towards her father or mother may be transferred to her husband.

```
0    1    2    3    4    5    6    7    8    9    10
L____|____|____|____|____|____|____|____|____|____|
```

Your Mother Is Repulsed by Your Father

The characteristics that attracted her to her husband early in their relationship become the very things that repulse her from him after the marriage. She does not understand her own feelings about this drastic change in her attitudes.

```
0    1    2    3    4    5    6    7    8    9    10
L____|____|____|____|____|____|____|____|____|____|
```

Your Mother Is Insecure

She has a tendency to be terribly insecure. If she is a Christian, she often doubts her salvation. She is prone toward having many anxieties and is often depressed.

```
0    1    2    3    4    5    6    7    8    9    10
L____|____|____|____|____|____|____|____|____|____|
```

Your Mother Has a Lesbian Tendency

She will particularly show this tendency if the "absent-mother" condition was a critical factor in her childhood years. She will be attracted to older women as her need for a mother's affection expresses itself.

```
0    1    2    3    4    5    6    7    8    9    10
L____|____|____|____|____|____|____|____|____|____|
```

Your Mother Has Boyish Behavior

Sometimes she will adopt male characteristics in an attempt to gain her father's attention and approval. This is particularly the case if she discovers that her father was disappointed that she was not born male.

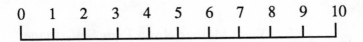

```
0   1   2   3   4   5   6   7   8   9   10
L___I___I___I___I___I___I___I___I___I___I
```

Your Mother Rationalizes

She tends to rationalize immoral behavior, especially if necessary to offset her inner guilt feelings. (I have often heard women say, "Anything that feels this good cannot be wrong.")

```
0   1   2   3   4   5   6   7   8   9   10
L___I___I___I___I___I___I___I___I___I___I
```

Your Mother Is Deceived

She can easily deceive herself into believing an immoral relationship is God's will for her. She will even justify abandoning her children as she pursues her own selfish interests.

```
0   1   2   3   4   5   6   7   8   9   10
L___I___I___I___I___I___I___I___I___I___I
```

Your Mother Has Maturity Problems

She tends to be immature in relating to other men, especially older men. She does this in a continued attempt to be "daddy's little girl" to them, still craving the love and affirmation not provided during her critical childhood years.

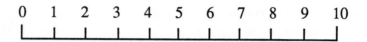

Your Mother Has a Poor Self-Image

She tends to feel she is not feminine, and will question her womanhood. She may be promiscuous to prove her sexuality. She lacks a sense of personal worth, feeling both inadequate and unattractive.

0   1   2   3   4   5   6   7   8   9   10

Your Mother Is Intelligent

She has a brilliant mind and she may tend to feel superior to her husband.

0   1   2   3   4   5   6   7   8   9   10

Your Mother Is Controlling

She seeks to tightly control every aspect of her life. This control can be quite strong, even to the point of possessiveness.

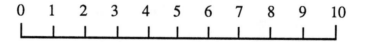

Your Mother Has a Desire for Paternal Affection

She is driven by a desire to satisfy her needs for paternal affection. She will attempt to meet them through her husband, but if that fails, she will try to meet them in other relationships. She can be quite aggressive sexually. She can become bitter toward her husband when he fails to give her the attention and affection she wants.

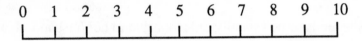

Your Mother Is Sexually Aggressive

She is flirtatious, impudent, and promiscuous.

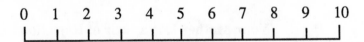

Your Mother Is Indecisive

She will readily make decisions in some areas of her life but will be maddeningly indecisive in other areas.

$$0 \quad 1 \quad 2 \quad 3 \quad 4 \quad 5 \quad 6 \quad 7 \quad 8 \quad 9 \quad 10$$

Your Mother "Mothers" Your Father

She will not view herself as an adequate mother. However, if she is from an "absent-mother" background, her motherly instincts may be quite strong. A girl with strong motherly instincts is almost always attracted to a man who is either from a similar background or who has been doted upon by a possessive mother.

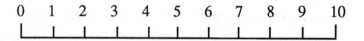

Your Mother Is Sexually Frigid

She tends to be sexually unresponsive to her husband. However, she is quite vulnerable to outside influences, especially older men who are father figures. She will almost always feel that she is falling in love with her counselor or pastor. (A great number of the "affairs" which destroy the ministries of pastors are with such women.)

0   1   2   3   4   5   6   7   8   9   10

Your Mother Is Expressive

She tends to be very creative and expressive. She normally will outshine her husband in group settings.

0   1   2   3   4   5   6   7   8   9   10

Your Mother Has a Fear of Rejection

She fears rejection more than anything else. She calculates what she says, how she dresses, where she goes, and who her friends are in order to be accepted by others. She has a tendency to fear men in authority, seeing them as a threat to her security.

0   1   2   3   4   5   6   7   8   9   10

Your Mother Is Gregarious

She tends to be vivacious and open, warm and outgoing, but she may smother people at the same time.

```
0   1   2   3   4   5   6   7   8   9   10
```

Your Mother Is Emotionally Traumatized

She often feels that if she stays in her marriage, she will lose her mind. At this point, she will either seek a separation or a divorce.

```
0   1   2   3   4   5   6   7   8   9   10
```

Your Mother Has a Little Girl Attitude

Around men, she will quite often become the flirtatious "little girl" or "little sister." She can be extremely naive in not knowing how she tantalizes men by this behavior. But if a man responds to her teasing by making advances, she will be shocked by his actions.

```
0   1   2   3   4   5   6   7   8   9   10
```

Your Mother Has a Revulsion Toward Sex

This is a tendency to have an unconscious revulsion toward sex with her husband. It occurs when the husband-wife relationship becomes more like a father-daughter relationship. Her attitude is like a daughter's revulsion toward a father in an incestuous situation.

```
0   1   2   3   4   5   6   7   8   9   10
```

Your Mother Is Self-Centered

She will find ways to be the center of attraction. This is especially true if she is the youngest or the only child.

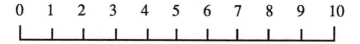

Your Mother Is Seductive

Men are objects to be conquered by her. She is not driven by a sexual lust, but by a determination to dominate men.

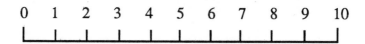

Your Mother Has Character Strength

She will seem to have a greater strength of character than her husband, but instead of affirming her weaker mate, she criticizes him for being a wimp.

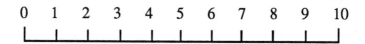

Your Mother Is Self-Condemning

She usually takes all the blame and has a martyr complex, but she still deeply desires to have a relationship with a man. Battered wives nearly always have this symptom.

Your Mother Is Promiscuous

She has a tendency to seek in many men the affection and attention not provided by her father. She is attracted to older men. She will trade sex for being held by a man, but she may not view herself as being promiscuous.

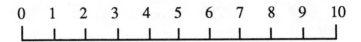

Your Mother Compares Her Husband to Other Men

She compares her husband to other men, always wondering if she might have married someone better than him.

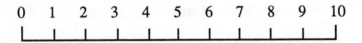

Your Mother Has High Expectations

She has very high expectations for the people in her home. She demands high levels of performance from her husband and children. She has a tendency to nag and be critical of them.

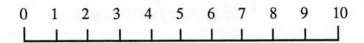

Your Mother Is Hostile

She often expresses anger at her husband, and she can be quite unreasonable. He may not attempt to stop her, because he has learned that trying to calm her only increases the problem. This type of anger is called "intimidating anger."

0   1   2   3   4   5   6   7   8   9   10

Your Mother Is Driven

She will try to accomplish all that she possibly can in a given period of time. As a result, she is admired because she is able to do more than most women.

0   1   2   3   4   5   6   7   8   9   10

Your Mother Is a Hoarder

Because of deeply rooted insecurities, she has difficulty in getting rid of anything. She keeps items until her husband is totally frustrated by her hoarding. Then serious conflict can ensue over things like old magazines or used bottles.

0   1   2   3   4   5   6   7   8   9   10

Your Mother Is a High Achiever

She is performance-oriented. Self-imposed laws and high expectations drive her to become a workaholic. She may be overly active in church, the P.T.A., clubs, etc.

0   1   2   3   4   5   6   7   8   9   10

Your Mother Is Demanding

She will often demand her "rights" from her husband and others. She tends to be domineering and pushy.

```
0   1   2   3   4   5   6   7   8   9   10
```

Your Mother Is Resistant

She will resist her husband in any attempt he might make to enrich or increase their interpersonal relationships. Ultimately, he may view her as someone to fear, and will "walk on eggshells" when he's near her.

```
0   1   2   3   4   5   6   7   8   9   10
```

Your Mother Lives by Feelings

She tends to live by her feelings. She is very moody.

```
0   1   2   3   4   5   6   7   8   9   10
```

Your Mother Has Been Abused

She may have a history of being sexually abused as a child, either by her father or by other men who took advantage of her.

```
0   1   2   3   4   5   6   7   8   9   10
```

Your Mother Is Selectively Submissive

She complains that her husband will not take a leadership role in their marriage, but she resists and ridicules him when he makes attempts to do so. She becomes submissive only in the areas of her choosing.

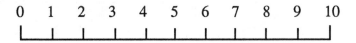

Your Mother Is Mistrusting

She doesn't trust her husband to handle important details responsibly. She feels she can do a better job. For example, she will often handle the family finances by controlling the checkbook.

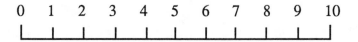

Your Mother Excludes Your Father

She tends to ignore her husband and not make time to meet his needs. She creates a world of her own with her children. Often, the husband will react by becoming absent from the home much more than necessary.

0   1   2   3   4   5   6   7   8   9   10

Your Mother Is Outwardly Clean

She is very neat and clean outwardly, but is quite sloppy where it doesn't show. The public areas of the house may look immaculate, but the bedrooms, closets, etc., are disaster areas. Her personal grooming may betray a penchant to "look good" to others, but be unkempt during private family times.

```
0   1   2   3   4   5   6   7   8   9   10
L___I___I___I___I___I___I___I___I___I___J
```

Your Mother Is Frustrated

She often feels trapped in her relationship with her husband. Her frustration increases when her attempts to control him become thwarted. Her husband often seeks to offset his wife's determination to control him by becoming unresponsive and even more passive. This, in turn, creates more problems in their relationship.

```
0   1   2   3   4   5   6   7   8   9   10
L___I___I___I___I___I___I___I___I___I___J
```

Your Mother Has Role Confusion

She has difficulty in distinguishing between her father and her husband. This is usually the case when she marries to get her needs for paternal affection met, which causes sexual hang-ups in her marriage. Such a woman may, on occasions, find sexual relationships outside of her marriage easier to handle. In that case, she does not have the guilt of going to bed with her "father."

```
0   1   2   3   4   5   6   7   8   9   10
L___I___I___I___I___I___I___I___I___I___J
```

Your Mother Is Impulsive

She spends large amounts of money on impulse, or she makes decisions which are not thought through with care. She may use charge accounts so irresponsibly that her husband closes all of them as a means to protect himself from bankruptcy.

```
0   1   2   3   4   5   6   7   8   9   10
|___|___|___|___|___|___|___|___|___|___|
```

Your Mother Has Anorexic and Bulimic Tendencies

Eating disorders may be manifestations of her unmet cravings for a father's love and affection.

```
0   1   2   3   4   5   6   7   8   9   10
|___|___|___|___|___|___|___|___|___|___|
```

Your Mother Creates Interpersonal Crisis

She deliberately creates crises within her home, especially when the husband is stoic and non-communicative. Like little children who cannot gain attention until they do something bad, she settles for anger from her husband as a better alternative than no response from him at all.

```
0   1   2   3   4   5   6   7   8   9   10
|___|___|___|___|___|___|___|___|___|___|
```

Your Mother Has a Poor Concept of God the Father

She has transferred her feelings about her earthly father to her feelings about God the Father. As a result, she may actually avoid thinking of God as Father.

```
0   1   2   3   4   5   6   7   8   9   10
|___|___|___|___|___|___|___|___|___|___|
```

Your Mother Doesn't Respect Your Father

She does not respect her husband, and she may have transferred to him her hostility toward her father. She finds it difficult to recognize this transference, and may deny this symptom exists if she is confronted with this concept.

```
0   1   2   3   4   5   6   7   8   9   10
```

Your Mother Has Emotional Instability

She is afraid of failure and intensely fears rejection. She may be withdrawn or calculated, or she may be prone to "renegade emotions." She may sometimes give license to these feelings and go on a spree: shopping, spending, drinking, etc.

```
0   1   2   3   4   5   6   7   8   9   10
```

Your Mother Has a Strong Emotional Makeup

She will be stronger in her emotional makeup than her husband, and she may be willing to admit that their marriage needs help. She will seek counseling, even when her husband will not. He may react to this situation by having an affair with a young woman whose emotional makeup is as weak as his own.

```
0   1   2   3   4   5   6   7   8   9   10
```

Your Mother Is Dependent on Other Men

She is dependent on other men, but may be rebellious to her husband.

She may complain to another man that her husband is not adequate for her.

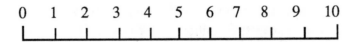

0   1   2   3   4   5   6   7   8   9   10

Your Mother Is Manipulative

She seeks to control situations by manipulating people. She may cause two people to become angry with each other, stepping back "in all innocence" to watch the fight she started by her gossip.

0   1   2   3   4   5   6   7   8   9   10

Your Mother Relates Better to Men Than to Women

She does not have many female friends. Her best relationships are with men. She may not be immoral in any of these contacts. She simply feels more comfortable conversing with men than women. She may excuse this by remarking that "women are so shallow."

0   1   2   3   4   5   6   7   8   9   10

How Have These Symptoms Affected You?

Go back through each of your responses in this section and answer the following questions:

1. Which traits concerning your *mother* were evident (seven or more on the scale)? List these:

_____

_____

_____

_____

_____

_____

_____

_____

_____

_____

2. How have each of these affected you? Be specific.

_____

_____

_____

_____

_____

_____

_____

_____

_____

_____

3. Do you see any of these traits (those you listed in questions 1 and 2) in your life, your marriage, or your relationship with your children? If so, which ones?

_____

_____

_____

_____

_____

_____

_____

_____

_____

_____

_____

_____

As you completed Step Five, you may have wondered, *Is there a cure for what this has done to me?*

Yes! Though the development of our belief system took place unconsciously, we can now deliberately start to change it. Step Seven will help you begin to accomplish this goal.

THE NAMES OF GOD

The more we understand God's character, the more we will trust Him. Throughout the Bible, the various names of God specifically reveal an aspect of the character of God. Though our Bibles usually don't use these descriptive names, it is helpful for us to study them so that we can apply specific characteristics of God to our specific needs. This step is designed to facilitate that study.

In Chapter Seven, the names of God are listed and described. Go through that chapter and write a definition for each one in the space provided in this step. Then describe some circumstances in your life (present, past, or future) when each name and characteristic would help you.

For example:

ELOHIM
Definition: *unlimited strength, energy, might and power; to make a covenant.*

Circumstances: *When I was unsure of my salvation, I realized that God had promised to forgive me and make me His child if I would accept Christ's death as the payment for my sins. I realized that my faith could be based on His promise.*

I need the Lord to give me strength to relate to my boss in a way that honors Him. He has promised to provide the wisdom and strength I need.

ELOHIM

Definition:_____

Circumstances:_____

_____

_____

_____

_____

_____

JEHOVAH

Definition:_____

Circumstances:_____

_____

_____

_____

_____

_____

ADONAI

Definition:_____

Circumstances:_____

_____

_____

_____

_____

_____

EL SHADDAI

Definition:_____

_____

Circumstances:_____

_____

_____

_____

_____

_____

EL ELYON

Definition:_____

_____

Circumstances:_____

_____

_____

_____

_____

_____

EL OLAM

Definition:_____

_____

Circumstances:_____

_____

_____

_____

_____

_____

EL ROI

Definition:_____

_____

Circumstances:_____

_____

_____

_____

_____

_____

JEHOVAH-JIREH

Definition:_____

_____

Circumstances:_____

_____

_____

_____

_____

_____

JEHOVAH-NISSI

Definition:_____

_____

Circumstances:_____

_____

_____

_____

_____

_____

JEHOVAH-TSIDKENU

Definition:_____

_____

Circumstances:_____

_____

_____

_____

_____

JEHOVAH-RAAH

Definition:_____

_____

Circumstances:_____

_____

_____

_____

_____

JEHOVAH-RAPHA

Definition:_____

_____

Circumstances:_____

_____

_____

_____

_____

JEHOVAH-SHALOM

Definition:_____

_____

Circumstances:_____

_____

_____

_____

_____

_____

JEHOVAH-SABBAOTH

Definition:_____

_____

Circumstances:_____

_____

_____

_____

_____

_____

JEHOVAH-SHAMMAH

Definition:_____

_____

Circumstances:_____

_____

_____

_____

_____

_____

Which of these names of God is most meaningful to you?_____
Why?_____

_____
_____
_____
_____
_____
_____
_____
_____
_____

How will you apply that name to your circumstances today?

_____
_____
_____
_____
_____
_____
_____
_____
_____

It will be helpful for you to use these names for God as you pray.

LEARNING MORE ABOUT GOD
FROM PSALM 139

In addition to the names of God, there are passages in the Bible which highlight certain aspects of our relationship with God.

In Psalm 139, we have a perfect example of such passages. This Psalm describes the character of God in a number of ways. Studying it can help you understand how His omniscience, omnipresence, and omnipotence apply to you and your circumstances. (Some people underline passages of Scripture that are particularly meaningful to them. This is a good habit because it reinforces what they are learning. Why not use your pencil and your Bible as you study this Psalm?)

We will examine the Psalm a few verses at a time. Then we will ask questions to promote reflection and application.

God Knows Me Individually

Verses 1-4: *O Lord, you have searched me and you know me. You know when I sit and when I rise; you perceive my thoughts from afar. You discern my going out and my lying down; you are familiar with all my ways. Before a word is on my tongue you know it completely, O Lord.*

1. God always knows what you are going to say, and He loves you unconditionally! How does this make you feel?

_____

_____

2. In what ways does God's omniscience give you courage and strength?

_____
_____
_____
_____
_____
_____

He Knows My Situation Thoroughly

Verses 5-6: *You hem me in–behind and before; you have laid your hand upon me. Such knowledge is too wonderful for me, too lofty for me to attain.*

1. God's perfect knowledge about you enables Him to protect you (to hem you in). From what do you need His protection?

_____
_____
_____
_____
_____
_____

2. Are you amazed at the Lord's omniscience? Why or why not?

_____
_____
_____
_____
_____
_____

He Is Always Present

Verses 7-12: *Where can I go from your Spirit? Where can I flee from your presence? If I go up to the heavens, you are there; if I make my bed in the depths,* [Hebrew Sheol], *you are there. If I rise on the wings of the dawn, if I settle on the far side of the sea, even there your hand will guide me, your right hand will hold me fast. If I say, "Surely the darkness will hide me and the light become night around me," even the darkness will not be dark to you; the night will shine like the day, for darkness is as light to you.*

1. The most important assurance to one who has strayed is that he is not lost! How close is God to you?

_____

_____

_____

2. How close does He *seem* to be?

_____

_____

_____

3. How far can you get from Him?

_____

_____

_____

He Is a Sovereign Creator

Verses 13-15: *For you created my inmost being; you knit me together in my mother's womb. I praise you because I am fearfully and wonderfully made; your works are wonderful, I know that full well. My frame was not hidden from you when I was made in the secret place. When I was woven together in the depths of the earth...*

1. Who is responsible for your appearance?

_____

_____

_____

2.   *a*) Can you rejoice that you look exactly the way the Father wants you to look?

_____

b) If so, why?

_____
_____
_____
_____
_____

c) If not, why not?

_____
_____
_____
_____

d) How do you normally respond to your appearance?

_____
_____
_____

e) How should you respond to your appearance?

_____
_____
_____

3. Do you think (or worry) about what other people think of your appearance? Why or why not?

_____

_____

_____

4. How would this Psalm help free you from the fear of what others think of you?

_____

_____

_____

_____

God Has a Plan for You

Verse 16: *your eyes saw my unformed body. All the days ordained for me were written in your book before one of them came to be.*

1. List as many obvious aspects of God's plan for you as you can think of:
Examples:

He wants me to love and forgive others.

He wants me to pray and study His word.

_____

_____

_____

_____

_____

_____

_____

God Is Constant and Consistent

Verses 17, 18: *How precious to me are your thoughts, O God! How vast is the sum of them! Were I to count them, they would outnumber the grains of sand. When I awake, I am still with you.*

1.   *a*) The Lord is infinite and He is thinking about you all the time! Describe how that fact comforts and encourages you:

_____

_____

_____

_____

_____

_____

_____

_____

The Response of Openness and Obedience

Verses 23, 24: *Search me, O God, and know my heart; test me and know my anxious thoughts. See if there is any offensive way in me, and lead me in the way everlasting.*

Openness to God's correction and guidance is the way the psalmist responds to the secure position he has with God. You also have a secure position with God, through Jesus, who died to pay for your sins and rose from the dead to give you new life.

1.   *a*) Are you open to God's correction and guidance?_____

    b) Why, or why not?

_____

_____

_____

_____

Conclusion:

You have taken another step toward developing a special, distinct category for your relationship with God. You now know Him by His name, and you're becoming familiar with His ways. That's just a start!

Think of how many years, how many experiences it took for you to create a category for earthly fathers. A strong understanding of your Heavenly Father will require time, study, and experiences with Him.

CHILDREN OF GOD

To be a child of God is the greatest privilege anyone can experience, yet we often use the term flippantly, without reflecting on what it means to be God's child. This step is designed to help you reflect on the truths of your identity as a child of God.

The Basis of the Relationship

Look at each passage and describe what was true of you *before* you became a child of God and what is true of you *now* as a child of God.

Col. 1:19-22

For it was the Father's good pleasure for all the fulness to dwell in Him, and through Him to reconcile all things to Himself, having made peace through the blood of His cross; through Him, I say, whether things on earth or things in heaven. And although you were formerly alienated and hostile in mind, engaged in evil deeds, yet He has now reconciled you in His fleshly body through death, in order to present you before Him holy and blameless and beyond reproach...

Before:

_____

_____

_____

Now:

_____

_____

_____

Rom. 5:6-11

For while we were still helpless, at the right time Christ died for the ungodly. For one will hardly die for a righteous man; though perhaps for the good man someone would dare even to die. But God demonstrates His own love toward us, in that while we were yet sinners, Christ died for us. Much more then, having now been justified by His blood, we shall be saved from the wrath of God through the death of His Son, much more, having been reconciled, we shall be saved by His life. And not only this, but we also exult in God through our Lord Jesus Christ, through whom we have now received the reconciliation.

Before:

_____

_____

_____

Now:

_____

_____

_____

Titus 3:3-7

For we also once were foolish ourselves, disobedient, deceived, enslaved to various lusts and pleasures, spending our life in malice and envy, hateful, hating one another. But when the kindness of God our Savior and His love for mankind appeared, He saved us, not on the basis of deeds which we have done in righteousness, but according to His mercy, by the washing of regeneration and renewing by the Holy Spirit, whom He poured out upon us richly through Jesus Christ our Savior, that being justified by His grace we might be made heirs according to the hope of eternal life.

Before:

_____

_____

_____

Now:

_____

_____

_____

The Nature of the Relationship

Paraphrase each passage, then describe God's role in the relationship and our response to Him.

Rom. 8:14-17

For all who are being led by the Spirit of God, these are sons of God. For you have not received a spirit of slavery leading to fear again, but you have received a spirit of adoption as sons by which we cry out, "Abba! Father!" The Spirit Himself bears witness with our spirit that we are children of God, and if children, heirs also, heirs of God and fellow heirs with Christ, if indeed we suffer with Him in order that we may also be glorified with Him.

Paraphrase:

_____

_____

_____

_____

_____

God's Role:

_____
_____
_____

Our Response:

_____
_____
_____

1 John 3:1-3

See how great a love the Father has bestowed upon us, that we should be called children of God; and such we are. For this reason the world does not know us, because it did not know Him. Beloved, now we are children of God, and it has not appeared as yet what we shall be. We know that, when He appears, we shall be like Him, because we shall see Him just as He is. And everyone who has this hope fixed on Him purifies himself, just as He is pure.

Paraphrase:

_____
_____
_____
_____
_____
_____

God's Role:

_____
_____
_____

Our Response:

_____

_____

_____

Matt. 7:7-11

Ask, and it shall be given to you; seek, and you shall find; knock, and it shall be opened to you. For everyone who asks receives, and he who seeks finds, and to him who knocks it shall be opened. Or what man is there among you, when his son shall ask him for a loaf, will give him a stone? Or if he shall ask for a fish, he will not give him a snake, will he? If you then, being evil, know how to give good gifts to your children, how much more shall your Father who is in heaven give what is good to those who ask Him!

Paraphrase:

_____

_____

_____

_____

_____

God's Role:

_____

_____

Our Response:

_____

_____

_____

Eph. 2:11-22

Therefore remember, that formerly you, the Gentiles in the flesh, who are called "Uncircumcision" by the so-called "Circumcision," which is performed in the flesh by human hands—remember that you were at that time separate from Christ, excluded from the commonwealth of Israel, and strangers to the covenants of promise, having no hope and without God in the world. But now in Christ Jesus you who formerly were far off have been brought near by the blood of Christ. For He Himself is our peace, who made both groups into one, and broke down the barrier of the dividing wall, by abolishing in His flesh the enmity, which is the Law of commandments contained in ordinances, that in Himself He might make the two into one new man, thus establishing peace, and might reconcile them both in one body to God through the cross, by it having put to death the enmity. And He came and preached peace to you who were far away, and peace to those who were near; for through Him we both have our access in one Spirit to the Father. So then you are no longer strangers and aliens, but you are fellow citizens with the saints, and are of God's household, having been built upon the foundation of the apostles and prophets, Christ Jesus Himself being the corner stone, in whom the whole building, being fitted together is growing into a holy temple in the Lord; in whom you also are being built together into a dwelling of God in the Spirit.

Paraphrase:

_____

_____

_____

_____

_____

_____

God's Role:

_____

_____

_____

Our Response:

_____

_____

_____

Conclusion:

1. Write a summary paragraph about God's role in your relationship with Him. What has He accomplished? How does He feel and act toward you?

_____

_____

_____

_____

_____

_____

_____

_____

_____

_____

_____

_____

_____

_____

_____

2. How have you perceived God in the past?

_____

_____

_____

_____

_____

_____

3. Has this study begun to change this perception? If so, how?

_____

_____

_____

_____

_____

4. How can you respond to the Lord more appropriately this week? Be specific.

_____

_____

_____

_____

_____

_____

_____

_____

_____

_____

_____

_____

_____

_____

OVERCOMING
EMOTIONAL ROADBLOCKS

"Why do I act this way?"

"Why can't I ever feel secure and happy?"

"I feel numb. I know I should feel angry or happy or sad, but I just feel numb."

"Why am I so volatile?"

"Why do I give in so readily? I am so easily manipulated!"

"I treat my children the same way my parents treated me–and I hate it!"

These and many other questions and statements are expressions of profound desperation. Many of us have developed strong defense mechanisms to block emotional pain and to win the approval of others. Some of us are driven to succeed. Some of us have only selective memories. Some are emotionally numb, or sullen and depressed, and some withdraw from others. While some of us seem to be even-tempered most of the time, we may occasionally explode in anger. These emotional roadblocks prevent us from enjoying intimacy with God and serving the Lord in a dynamic, fruitful way.

To overcome these roadblocks, we need to go to the source: the painful events that caused the hurt. Then we can experience the hurt, feel the anger, grieve over our loss, and accept the Lord's grace even in the midst of our pain. This process does not yield instantaneous results. The procedure can be long, but it does result in hope and healing.

In Chapter Eleven, "What Do I Do with My Emotions?" we looked at the stages a person goes through as he comes to grips with emotional trauma. Let's briefly review those stages:

Denial: A defense designed to block pain by either suppressing the hurt–rationalizing that the conflict was our fault in an attempt to avoid blaming our parents–or avoiding painful emotions in some other way.

Anger: When a person begins to feel the pain that has been suppressed (often for many years), he usually becomes very angry with the one who has hurt him.

Bargaining: Our first response to the reality of hurt, neglect, and condemnation is to bargain. We try to make a deal. *What can I do to get him to love me?* But the bargaining stage still isn't completely objective. (Bargaining may be triggered by the initial awareness of hurt and anger. The process of bargaining, however, usually precedes a deeper awareness of hurt and anger, so bargaining is, in effect, sandwiched between pain and anger. The entire process, as you may recall, doesn't follow a rigid schedule. There are many movements forward and backward over the various stages as new insights are seen.)

Grief: After a time of anger, the person's indignation abates and a sense of loss prevails. He realizes that he has lost the chance to have a happy childhood or a close relationship with his parents. He experiences deep sorrow over the qualities of life he has never had; qualities like love, intimacy and security.

Acceptance: Sooner or later, the process of grieving for these losses is over, and though the person may have periods of anger and grief from time to time, he can accept that a loving and sovereign God has a perfect plan for his life. Now he can begin to experience the intimacy and warmth of God and other people previously blocked by his defense mechanism(s).

Step Nine is an introduction to this process. For many people, it is a pivotal step, and it may provide the framework for the healing they so desperately need from the Lord. Before you begin to apply the principles that will help you through these stages, there are some additional ideas that can aid you:

1. Don't rush the process. It will take more than an hour or a day to dig through the defense mechanisms you have erected. You may have suppressed hurt and anger for twenty, thirty, forty years or more. Don't expect too much too soon. Take time to reflect and to experience the hurt and anger you have suppressed. Then, take time to feel the sorrow in the grief process. You will experience a gradual healing throughout these stages. The entire process may well take months (or even years!), but it is worth it.

2. Throughout the process, you will become aware of a growing sense of objectivity. Defense mechanisms may protect us from pain, but they blind us to the truth. Some people will realize that they felt guilty (instead of hurt) when their parents shouted at them. These people felt responsible for their parents' happiness, and when their parents weren't happy, they felt it was their fault.

Some people will realize that, apart from divine intervention, their parents will *never* love and affirm them, no matter how hard they try to please them.

With this objectivity will come a new sense of identity. The bondage to parental approval can be slowly broken, and a healthy sense of independence can be developed.

3. As you begin to experience and express your new identity, it is quite possible that your parents and siblings may not like it at all. As long as you played your role in the family, they were in control. But your new identity may threaten their control, and they may respond with more condemnation and manipulation than ever! Be prepared for *more* conflict, not less.

4. The grief process over the loss you have experienced is an unusual one because the loss is intangible. There is no actual corpse, but the death of a child's identity through neglect or manipulation is a very real loss.

Normally, the grief process has a specific beginning (when someone dies), and it ends when the emotion is fully expressed. In this case, however, you may have to continue relating to the one who caused the hurt; therefore, the sense of grief may need to be experienced again and again. These subsequent experiences will be less painful if the initial process of going through the stages is deep, profound, and cathartic.

5. Learning to respond with a new identity (especially responding to those who have hurt you deeply) is much like learning to ride a bicycle. No six year old gets off his tricycle, hops on a 26" ten-speed, and rides around the neighborhood with no problem! A person learns to ride a bike by trying...and falling...and trying again, going a little farther...and falling again. Turns and hills present new challenges...and new falls.

Be realistic about your progress. Don't expect perfection! Responding with your new identity is at first as awkward and scary as it is to get on a bike for the first time. But after a while, and after a lot of practice, it gets easier.

6. Be prepared for the battle by fortifying your mind and heart with the encouragement of the Scriptures. The chapter and step on the "Names of God," the chapter on "Children of God," and the step on "Characteristics of Christ" will help you learn the truth about the Lord and about your new identity.

Take time to study, to reflect, and to memorize. It will be well worth the trouble! (And the consequences of *not* doing it are severe.)

7. The experience of overcoming denial and experiencing hurt, anger, and grief is a painful ordeal. A loving and faithful friend can help you endure this process. There will be times when you will need a fresh perspective, some objective wisdom, strong encouragement, or a warm hug of reassurance. Find someone who understands what you're going through and who will be a true friend to you.

The first several steps in this workbook are designed to help you overcome denial by understanding how your parents related to each other, how they related to you, and how they affected your view of God.

Perhaps these exercises have already awakened some repressed emotions in you. The next section will help you go through another step in the process.

Awareness, Hurt, and Anger

When you aren't hurried, find a quiet place where you won't be disturbed. Ask the Lord to remind you of specific instances in your past, particularly your childhood, when you experienced hurt, anger, or guilt because of your parents. Some of these events will probably come to mind very quickly, but others may not. You may have a lull of twenty to thirty minutes before the Lord reminds you of another instance or two, and then another period of time before you remember another one. Make a list of these events until your memory's "well has run dry."

List and briefly describe those events here:

1. _____
   _____

2. _____
   _____

3. _____
   _____

4. _____
   _____

5. _____
   _____

6. _____
   _____

7. _____
   _____

8. _____
   _____

9. _____
   _____

10. _____
    _____

11. _____
    _____

12. _____
    _____

13. _____
    _____

14. _____
    _____

15. _____
    _____

(Use additional sheets of paper if necessary.)

Now, go back and describe these events in more detail. For instance:

Event:

> *My mother made me wear a new dress to school. It didn't fit. I felt ugly and the other girls laughed at me.*

The emotion I felt:
> *I cried, I felt ashamed, humiliated. I was angry at my mother.*

My actions:
> *I tried to avoid people all day. I went to the restroom to cry. I didn't say anything to my mother because she would have laughed at me and then she would have been mad at me.*

How a "normal" child (person) would have responded:
> *I think most little girls could have told their mothers that they didn't want to wear the dress because the other girls would laugh at them. Their mothers would respond by being reasonable and loving. They wouldn't demand that they wear a dress like that.*

How do you feel about the event and the person now?
> *I am really mad at my mother. She wasn't reasonable or loving. She only wanted her way. She didn't care about my feelings at all.*

What lie(s) were you believing?
> *Those who fail are unworthy of love and deserve to be blamed and condemned. Fear of punishment.*

Forgiveness Response:
> *I need to forgive my mother.*

Event:
> *I was hit in the head with a baseball bat, and my forehead bled a lot.*

The emotions I felt:
> *I refused to cry because my father never let me cry.*

My actions:

> *My friends tried to get me to go home, but I stayed in the game even though blood got in my eyes and all over my uniform.*

How a "normal" child (person) would have responded:

> *I would have cried and gone home to let my father comfort me and put a bandage on the cut.*

How do you feel about the event and the person now?

> *I'm hurt. My father was always tough with me. He never cried and he wouldn't let me cry. Now I don't feel emotions very much because of him. I've blocked my feelings all my life.*

What lie(s) were you believing?

> *I must meet certain standards to feel good about myself. I must be approved by certain others to feel good about myself.*

Forgiveness Response:

> *I need to forgive my father.*

As you go through this exercise, remember to relive the event, but this time don't suppress the emotions or try to change them. Express them fully to the Lord (Ps. 62:8).

1. Event:

_____

_____

_____

The emotions I felt:

_____

_____

_____

My actions:

_____
_____
_____

How a "normal" child would have responded:

_____
_____
_____

How do you feel about the event and the person now?

_____
_____
_____

What lie(s) were you believing?

_____
_____
_____

Forgiveness Response:

_____
_____
_____

2. Event:

_____
_____
_____

The emotions I felt:

_____
_____
_____

My actions:

_____
_____
_____

How a "normal" child would have responded:

_____
_____
_____

How do you feel about the event and the person now?

_____
_____
_____

What lie(s) were you believing?

_____
_____
_____

Forgiveness Response:

_____
_____
_____

3. Event:

_____
_____
_____

The emotions I felt:

_____
_____
_____

My actions:

_____

_____

_____

How a "normal" child would have responded:

_____

_____

_____

How do you feel about the event and the person now?

_____

_____

_____

What lie(s) were you believing?

_____

_____

_____

Forgiveness Response:

_____

_____

_____

4. Event:

_____

_____

_____

The emotions I felt:

_____

_____

_____

My actions:

_____
_____
_____

How a "normal" child would have responded:

_____
_____
_____

How do you feel about the event and the person now?

_____
_____
_____

What lie(s) were you believing?

_____
_____
_____

Forgiveness Response:

_____
_____
_____

5. Event:

_____
_____
_____

The emotions I felt:

_____
_____
_____

My actions:

_____

_____

_____

How a "normal" child would have responded:

_____

_____

_____

How do you feel about the event and the person now?

_____

_____

_____

What lie(s) were you believing?

_____

_____

_____

Forgiveness Response:

_____

_____

_____

6. Event:

_____

_____

_____

The emotions I felt:

_____

_____

_____

My actions:

_____

_____

_____

How a "normal" child would have responded:

_____

_____

_____

How do you feel about the event and the person now?

_____

_____

_____

What lie(s) were you believing?

_____

_____

_____

Forgiveness Response:

_____

_____

_____

7. Event:

_____

_____

_____

The emotions I felt:

_____

_____

_____

My actions:

_____

_____

_____

How a "normal" child would have responded:

_____

_____

_____

How do you feel about the event and the person now?

_____

_____

_____

What lie(s) were you believing?

_____

_____

_____

Forgiveness Response:

_____

_____

_____

8. Event:

_____

_____

_____

The emotions I felt:

_____

_____

_____

My actions:

_____

_____

_____

How a "normal" child would have responded:

_____

_____

_____

How do you feel about the event and the person now?

_____

_____

_____

What lie(s) were you believing?

_____

_____

_____

Forgiveness Response:

_____

_____

_____

9. Event:

_____

_____

_____

The emotions I felt:

_____

_____

_____

My actions:

_____

_____

_____

How a "normal" child would have responded:

_____

_____

_____

How do you feel about the event and the person now?

_____

_____

_____

What lie(s) were you believing?

_____

_____

_____

Forgiveness Response:

_____

_____

_____

10. Event:

_____

_____

_____

The emotions I felt:

_____

_____

_____

My actions:

_____

_____

_____

How a "normal" child would have responded:

_____

_____

_____

How do you feel about the event and the person now?

_____

_____

_____

What lie(s) were you believing?

_____

_____

_____

Forgiveness Response:

_____

_____

_____

11. Event:

_____

_____

_____

The emotions I felt:

_____

_____

_____

My actions:

_____

_____

_____

How a "normal" child would have responded:

_____

_____

_____

How do you feel about the event and the person now?

_____

_____

_____

What lie(s) were you believing?

_____

_____

_____

Forgiveness Response:

_____

_____

_____

12. Event:

_____

_____

_____

The emotions I felt:

_____

_____

_____

My actions:

_____

_____

_____

How a "normal" child would have responded:

_____

_____

_____

How do you feel about the event and the person now?

_____

_____

_____

What lie(s) were you believing?

_____

_____

_____

Forgiveness Response:

_____

_____

_____

13. Event:

_____

_____

_____

The emotions I felt:

_____

_____

_____

My actions:

_____

_____

_____

How a "normal" child would have responded:

_____

_____

_____

How do you feel about the event and the person now?

_____

_____

_____

What lie(s) were you believing?

_____

_____

_____

Forgiveness Response:

_____

_____

_____

14. Event:

_____

_____

_____

The emotions I felt:

_____

_____

_____

My actions:

_____

_____

_____

How a "normal" child would have responded:

_____

_____

_____

How do you feel about the event and the person now?

_____

_____

_____

What lie(s) were you believing?

_____

_____

_____

Forgiveness Response:

_____

_____

_____

15. Event:

_____

_____

_____

The emotions I felt:

_____

_____

_____

My actions:

_____
_____
_____

How a "normal" child would have responded:

_____
_____
_____

How do you feel about the event and the person now?

_____
_____
_____

What lie(s) were you believing?

_____
_____
_____

Forgiveness Response:

_____
_____
_____

(Use additional paper if necessary.)

Bargaining

As you have become aware of the pain of your past, how have you tried to get your parents to give you the love and acceptance you have wanted? What have you said or done to win their approval?

_____
_____
_____

_____

_____

_____

Grief

After weeks or months of experiencing and expressing repressed anger, you will begin to grieve. Look at each of the events that you described on the previous pages.

1. What did you lose?

_____

_____

_____

2. What would a "normal" child have had that you didn't have?

_____

_____

_____

3. What do you wish you had received from your parents?

_____

_____

_____

4. How has your view of God been affected by your parents?

_____

_____

_____

5. How have your relationships been affected?

_____

_____

_____

6. How has your self-concept, identity, and confidence been affected?

_____

_____

_____

7. How do you feel about what you have lost?

_____

_____

_____

Acceptance

After you have experienced the hurt and anger for a while, you will then experience a sense of grief. After that, you will begin to see that God can develop a relationship with you that is intimate, warm, and powerful. Also, you will see that God has built strengths in your life through your pain.

1. How has your view of God changed as you have gone through this process?

_____

_____

_____

2. What strengths has God built into your life through your painful family experiences? (See Chapter Twelve, "Rivers in the Desert.")

_____

_____

_____

3. How has (and how will) God use these strengths to help others?

_____

_____

_____

4. What do you need to know, feel, and do when your parents and siblings don't understand your new identity, your new attitude, new independence, and new actions?

_____

_____

_____

Forgiveness

The process isn't complete until you have forgiven those who have hurt you. This forgiveness isn't easy, but it is an integral part of the stages of grief and acceptance.

1. Read Matt. 18, 1 John 4:9-11, Col. 3:13, and Rom. 15:7.
   *a)*What did your sins deserve?

_____

_____

_____

   *b)*How many of them did Christ die for?

_____

_____

_____

   c)How much does Christ love, forgive, and accept you?

_____

_____

_____

2. You can express to others only what you have experienced. Have you experienced Christ's healing love and forgiveness? If so, how?

_____

_____

_____

3. How can you express His love, forgiveness, and acceptance to those who have hurt you? Be specific:

_____
_____
_____
_____
_____
_____
_____
_____
_____
_____
_____
_____
_____
_____
_____
_____
_____
_____
_____
_____
_____
_____
_____
_____
_____
_____
_____
_____
_____
_____

MOTIVATIONS FOR OBEDIENCE

Our motivations are a product of our view of God, and as we have seen, our view of God has been strongly shaped by our relationship with our parents. If a child has been loved, accepted, and protected, he will be more likely to respond to his parents with respect, love, and joyful obedience.

If, on the other hand, a child has not enjoyed that kind of environment, he will either rebel against his parents or try desperately to please, obeying them to earn their love. Neither of these options is healthy.

As a person's perception of God and his identity as a child of God are changed and developed, his reasons to obey God are changed and developed, too. Rom. 8:15 states:

> *For you have not received a spirit of slavery leading to fear again, but you have received a spirit of adoption as sons by which we cry out, "Abba! Father!"*

1. Imagine yourself as the slave of a cruel master.
What would be some of your motivations to obey him?

_____
_____
_____
_____
_____
_____
_____

2. Now imagine that you are that same slave, but you have been bought by a wealthy, kind, and generous man who then gives you your freedom. With this new freedom, he also gives you a room in his mansion, his own clothes to wear, and a seat next to him at his table for as long as you live. As a crowning gesture of his affection and commitment to you, he asks you to be one of his children.

What would be some of your motivations to obey him?

_____

_____

_____

_____

3. Go back to Step Three, "Comparing Categories."

What are some characteristics of your father that you listed, both positive and negative?

_____

_____

_____

_____

4. Imagine that someone else had made this list of characteristics for his (or her) father. Would this person obey his (or her) father? (Try to be as objective as possible.)

If so, why?

_____

_____

_____

_____

If not, why not?

_____

_____

_____

_____

Because the Lord is like the wealthy, kind, and generous man who bought, freed, and adopted the slave, we can learn to respond to Him with thankfulness and joyful obedience. (The rest of this step is taken from Step Seven of *The Search For Significance Workbook*.)[1]

If God is fully pleased with us as a result of Christ's death on our behalf, then why should we desire to live for Him daily? This step will identify six biblical motivations for choosing to obey God rather than live in sin, rebellion, and self-effort. It will also examine some poor motivations for obeying God.

Six Reasons to Obey God

1. Sin is destructive.

Satan has effectively blinded man to the painful, damaging consequences of sin. The effects of sin are all around us, yet most people continue to indulge in the pleasure-seeking and rampant self-centeredness that cause so much anguish and pain. Satan contradicted God in the Garden when he said, *"You surely shall not die!"* (Gen. 3:4) Sin is pleasant, but only for a season. Sooner or later, it will have destructive effects.

Sin is destructive in many ways. Emotionally, we can experience the pain of guilt and shame and the fear of failure and punishment. Mentally, we can experience the anguish of flashbacks, and we can expend enormous amounts of time and energy thinking about our sins and rationalizing our guilt. Physically, we may suffer psychosomatic illnesses or experience pain through physical abuse. There is the possibility of unwanted pregnancy or a shattered family through immorality, loss of property, or even the loss of life. Relationally, we can alienate ourselves from others. Spiritually, we grieve the Holy Spirit, lose our testimony with others, and break our fellowship with God. The painful and destructive effects of sin are so profound that why we don't have an aversion to it is a mystery!

a) Read Jonah 1. List the results of Jonah's choice of disobedience to God.

_____

_____

_____

b) In what ways have you seen specific effects of a particular sin in your life?

_____

_____

_____

c) How can viewing sin as destructive be a motivation for being obedient to God?

_____

_____

_____

2. The Father will discipline us if we continue a habit of sin.

Read Heb. 12:5-11.

Our loving Father has given us the Holy Spirit to convict us of sin. Conviction is proof that we have become the sons of God. The Spirit's conviction is given in order to warn us that we are making choices without regard to either God's truth or the consequences of sin. If we choose to be unresponsive to the Holy Spirit, our Heavenly Father will discipline us in love. Many people do not understand the difference between discipline and punishment. This chart shows the profound differences:

	PUNISHMENT	DISCIPLINE
SOURCE:	God's Wrath	God's Love
PURPOSE:	To Avenge A Wrong	To Correct A Wrong
RELATIONAL RESULT:	Alienation	Reconciliation
PERSONAL RESULT:	Guilt	A Righteous Lifestyle
DIRECTED TOWARD:	Non-believers	His Children

Jesus bore all the punishment we deserved on the cross; therefore, we no longer need to fear punishment from God for our sins. We should seek to do what is right so that our Father will not have to correct us through discipline. But when we *are* disciplined, we should remember that God is correcting us out of His love. This discipline leads us to righteous performance which is a reflection of the righteousness of Christ.

From Heb. 12:5-11:

a) Do you sometimes confuse God's correction with punishment? If so, why?

_____

_____

_____

b) How can understanding God's discipline be a motivation for you?

_____

_____

_____

3. His commands for us are good.

God's commands are given for two good purposes: to protect us from the destructiveness of sin, and to direct us in a life of joy and fruitfulness. We have a wrong perspective if we only view God's commands as restrictions in our lives. Instead, we must realize that His commands are guidelines given so that we might enjoy life to the fullest. God's commands should never be considered as a means to gain His approval.

In today's society, we have lost the concept of doing something because it is the right thing to do. Instead, we do things in exchange for some reward or favor, or to avoid punishment. Wouldn't it be novel to do something simply because it's the right thing to do? God's commands are holy, right, and good. Therefore, since they have value in themselves, we should choose to obey God and follow His commands.

a) Read Rom. 7:12-14 and 1 John 5:3. How are God's commands described?

_____

_____

_____

_____

_____

b) Read Deut. 5:29 and 6:24. What are some results of obedience to God's commands?

_____

_____

_____

_____

_____

c) How can viewing God's commands as good be a motivation to you?

_____

_____

_____

_____

_____

4. We will receive rewards for obedience.

Our self-worth is not based on our performance and obedience; however, what we do (or don't do) has tremendous implications on the quality of our lives and our impact on others for Christ's sake. Disobedience results in: spiritual poverty, or a short-circuiting of intimate fellowship with the One who loves us so much that He died for us; confusion, guilt, and frustration; and an absence of spiritual power and desire to see people won to Christ and become disciples. On the other hand, responding to the love, grace, and power of Christ enables us to experience His love, joy, and strength as we minister to others, endure difficulties, and live for Him who has *"...called us out of darkness into His marvelous light."* (I Pet. 2:9) We are completely loved, forgiven, and accepted apart from our performance, but how we live is very important!

Read I Cor. 3:11-15, II Cor. 5:9-11, and Rev. 20:11. According to these passages, unbelievers will be judged and condemned at the Great White Throne of Judgment for rejecting Christ. Though believers will be spared from this condemnation, we will stand before the Judgment Seat of Christ to have our deeds tested. Deeds done for the Lord will be honored, but those deeds done for ourselves will be destroyed by fire. The Greek word to describe this judgment seat is the same word used to describe the platform an athlete stands on to receive his wreath of victory for winning his event. The judgment seat is for the reward of good deeds, not the punishment for sin.

This chart demonstrates some of the differences between the Judgment Seat of Christ and the Great White Throne Judgment.

	JUDGMENT SEAT OF CHRIST: (I Cor. 3:11-15)	GREAT WHITE THRONE (Rev. 20:11)
WHO WILL APPEAR:	Christians	Non-Christians
WHAT WILL BE JUDGED:	Our Deeds	Their Deeds
PERSONAL RESULT:	Reward	Condemnation
ULTIMATE RESULT:	Used to honor Christ	Cast out of God's presence into the lake of fire

Read I Cor. 9:24-27 and II Tim. 2:3-7; 4:7-8. How does receiving a reward become a motivation for obedience?

_____

_____

_____

_____

_____

5. The love of Christ compels us to obey.

An understanding of God's grace compels us to action because love motivates us to please the One who has so freely loved us. When we experience love, we usually respond by seeking to express our love in return. Our obedience to God is an expression of our love for Him (John 14:15, 21) because our love for God comes from an understanding of what Christ has accomplished for us on the cross (II Cor. 5:14,15). We love because He first loved us and clearly demonstrated His love at the cross (I John 4:16).

But why is this great motivating factor missing in so many lives? Simply because many people don't believe that God loves them unconditionally. They expect His love to be conditional, based on their ability to earn it.

Our experience of God's love is based on our perception: if we believe that He is demanding or aloof, we will not experience His love and tenderness; but, if we realize His love is tender and strong, we will be highly motivated to obey Him.

If a person believes that God is harsh and demanding, he will be angry with Him. It has been observed that people in open rebellion against God are angry with Him, and they will often go into detail about how God has let them down and how He really doesn't care about them.

Think of times that you have been rebellious toward God, and ask Him to reveal your thoughts about Him during those times. Then, reflect on His complete, tender, unconditional love for you.

Does the love of Christ compel you to obey Him? Why or why not?

_____
_____
_____
_____
_____
_____
_____

6. Obedience is an opportunity to honor God.

Each time we choose to obey, we express the righteousness we have in Christ. Our performance, then, becomes a reflection of who we are in Christ.

a) Read I Cor. 3:16-17 and I Pet. 2:9. How are you described?

_____
_____
_____
_____
_____

b) What purposes for our lives do these passages suggest?

_____
_____
_____
_____
_____

How Your Life Is Affected by These
Reasons to Obey God

1. How much are you motivated by each of these reasons? Reflect on these motivations and rate each one on a scale of 0 (no motivation to you at all) to 10 (a persistent, conscious, compelling motivation):

_____Sin is destructive.

_____The Father will discipline us if we continue in a habit of sin.

_____His commands for us are good.

_____We will receive rewards for obedience.

_____The love of Christ compels us to obey.

_____Obedience is an opportunity to honor God.

2. Do any of these seem "purer" or "higher" to you? If so, which ones? Why?

_____

_____

_____

_____

_____

3. Which of these do you need to concentrate on? What can you do to further develop this motivation?

_____

_____

_____

_____

_____

Improper Motivations for Obedience

Jesus repeatedly emphasized that He is concerned not only with what we do, but why we do it. The Pharisees obeyed many rules and regulations, but their hearts were far from the Lord.   Motives are important! These are a few poor motivations for obeying God and their possible results:

1. Someone will find out.

Many people obey God because they are afraid of what others will think of them if they don't. Allen went on church visitation because he feared what his Sunday school class would think if he didn't. Barbara was married, but wanted to go out with a man at work. She didn't because of what others might think.

There are problems with determining your behavior solely on the basis of other people. First, there are times when no one is watching. Maybe you'll find yourself on a business trip and you don't know anyone in the city. The motive to refrain from sin is missing, so you indulge in it.

This happens to many Christian businessmen. The second problem is that eventually your desire to disobey may exceed the peer pressure to obey. Then you'll have no reason to obey. Lastly, once someone has found out you've sinned, you no longer have a reason to obey. Sherry didn't sleep with her boyfriend for fear of what her mother would say if she found out. Later, Sherry did sleep with him and her mother found out. Sherry lost her motivation to obey, so she slept with him regularly. Obeying God because of others' opinions might work for a while, but it won't honor God or set you free...and eventually it won't work at all.

Is the "fear of someone finding out" a motivation for you to obey God? If it is, identify the specific sin you are trying to avoid. Then, go back over the six reasons to obey God to refresh your mind and heart about the proper motivations for obedience. Which of these proper motives seems to encourage you the most in regard to your specific sin?

_____

_____

_____

_____

_____

2. God will be angry with me.

Some people obey God because they think He will get angry with them if they don't obey. We've already discussed the difference in God's discipline and punishment, but to reiterate, God disciplines us out of love, not anger. His response to our sin is grief, not condemnation (Eph. 4:30). Hank was afraid that God would "zap" him if he did anything wrong, so he performed for God. He lived every day in fear of God's anger. Predictably, his relationship with the Lord was cold and mechanical. God doesn't want us to live in fear of His anger, but in response to His love. This produces joyful obedience instead of fear.

If you knew that God's response to your sin was grief instead of anger, would that affect your motivation to obey Him? Why or why not?

_____

_____

_____

_____

_____

3. I couldn't approve of myself if I didn't obey.

Some people obey God only because they want to live up to the standards they've set for themselves. They simply couldn't stand themselves if they didn't obey. Sadly, the idea of yielding their lives to a loving Lord is far from their minds. They are only trying to live up to their own standards, and if they don't meet those standards, they are ashamed. These people are more concerned with "do's and don'ts" than anything else. Instead of an intimate relationship with God, they see the Christian life as a ritual with the key emphasis on "don't break the rules." Of course, if these people succeed in keeping the rules, they are full of pride. They also tend to compare themselves with others, hoping to be accepted on the basis of being a little bit better than someone else.

Phillip was brought up in a strict church family. He was taught that it was a tragic sin to curse. All of Phillip's friends cursed, but he never did. "I could never do such a thing," said Phillip. He always secretly thought that he was better than his friends. The issue with Phillip was never what God wanted or God's love for him. Instead, it was the compulsion to live up to his own standards. Phillip needed to base his behavior on God and His Word, not on his own criteria. God gave us His commands out of love for us, and we are protected and set free as we obey Him.

What things are you not doing because you couldn't stand yourself if you did? What are you doing to obey God out of the motivation to meet your own standards?

_____

_____

_____

_____

_____

4. I'll obey to be blessed.

God doesn't swap marbles. If a person's sole motive to obey is to be blessed, it's simply an attempt to manipulate God. The underlying assumption is: *I've been good enough...bless me.* It's true we will reap what we sow. It's true that obedience keeps us within God's plan for us. But our decision to obey should never be based solely on God's rewarding us. Brian went to church so that God would bless his business, not because he wanted to worship God. Cheryl chose not to spread gossip about Diane because she had told God that she wouldn't tell anybody about Diane if He would get her the promotion she wanted.

Do you try to make deals with God? Why or why not?

_____

_____

_____

_____

A Final Word

Christ has freed us from the bondage of sin so that we can respond to Him in obedience. We have discussed six biblical motivations for us to be involved in good works:

1. Sin is destructive.
2. The Father will discipline us.
3. His commands for us are good.
4. We will receive rewards.
5. The love of Christ compels us to obey.
6. Obedience is an opportunity to honor God.

There are times when our feelings seem to get in the way of our obedience. We may want to indulge in some particular sin, or we may be afraid of failure or what someone might think of us. We may be selfish, or maybe just tired. But we should not hide behind bad feelings to excuse disobedience. The Lord never said pleasant emotions were a prerequisite for following Him. He said, *"If anyone wishes to come after Me, let him deny himself* (and the "right" to pleasant emotions), *and take up his cross daily, and follow Me."* (Luke 9:23) This doesn't mean we should deny that we have emotions. We should express them fully to the Lord, telling Him how we feel, and then act in faith on the Word of God. Spiritual growth, character development, and Christian service should not be held hostage by our emotions. God has given each of us a will, and we can choose to honor the Lord even in spite of our emotions.

In different situations, we will draw upon different motivations for obedience. Sometimes, we need to be reminded of the destructiveness of sin in order to choose righteousness. At other times, we are truly overwhelmed by the love of God and want to honor Him. No matter which motivation applies, it is our underlying motivation that determines if our actions are done to honor God or to selfishly make us more acceptable to others, God, or ourselves. Elisabeth Elliot, Christian speaker and author, says, "Sometimes, 'struggling' is a nice word for postponed obedience." [2]

a) Are you postponing obedience in any area of your life?

_____

_____

_____

_____

b) What steps of action do you need to take to obey the Lord?

_____

_____

_____

_____

As you realize the right motivation to obey the Lord, and as you are able to identify improper motivations in your life, you may think, *I've never done anything purely for the Lord in my whole life!* You may feel a sense of pain and remorse for your inappropriate motives. But don't sink into a state of morbid introspection, demeaning yourself for your past attitudes. There are two perspectives that will help you focus on the Lord and grow in a godly desire to honor Him.

First, as stated before, obedience from a right motivation is a choice. It is not based on how you feel. At any and every point in your life (like right now) you can actively, consciously choose to honor Christ. The Lord wants you to live by your godly choices, not by your fickle emotions. Develop a sense of intensity about this choice, as Paul wrote, *"...we have as our ambition...to be pleasing to Him."* (II Cor. 5:9)

Second, since your motives are a reflection of what you believe, they will change as your belief system changes. Consistently considering and applying God's truth will have a profound and far-reaching impact on your motives. As you reject Satan's lies, you will be *"transformed by the renewing of your mind...."* (Rom. 12:2) You will have an increasing desire to honor the One who loves you and purchased you by His own blood.

So, as an act of your will, choose to honor the Lord no matter what your emotions tell you, and consistently learn and apply the truths of God's Word so that these truths begin to pervade your thoughts. Your motives won't become totally pure until you see Him face to face (I John 3:2), but the better you know Him, the more you will see that He is worthy of your love, loyalty, and obedience.

[1]Robert S. McGee, *The Search For Significance* (Houston, TX: Rapha Publishing, 1987), pp. 202-213.

BREAKING THE CYCLE:

Modeling God's Character To Your Children

To the degree that we understand and experience God's love, forgiveness and power, we will be able to express these characteristics and model them to our children. The following step is designed to help you model the character of God to your children.

(If you don't have children, you may want to work on this step with your other family members, roommate, or friends in mind.)

1. Read Ex. 34:5-8. Is it fair for God to allow sin to be reproduced in our families? Why or why not?

_____

_____

_____

_____

2. Read Eph. 4:20-24. How does this process apply to modeling the character of God to your children? Be specific.

_____

_____

_____

_____

3. Read Joel 2:24-26. Does this passage give you hope about your relationship with your children? Why or why not?

_____

_____

_____

_____

4. *a)* Describe your self-concept. What do you think of yourself? What is the basis of your self-worth?

_____

_____

_____

_____

b) What difference would it make in your life and your relationship with your children if your self-concept was based on the unconditional love of God instead of on your performance and the opinions of others?

_____

_____

_____

_____

5. *a)* What is your purpose in life? If a friend were to observe your attitude and activities, what would he say your purpose in life is?

_____

_____

_____

_____

b) Does your purpose need to be changed? If so, how?

_____

_____

_____

_____

6. *a)* How would being thankful for your children affect your relationship with them?

_____

_____

_____

_____

b) How would responding in grief instead of anger, when they disobey, affect your relationship with them?

_____

_____

_____

_____

7. *a)* Write out your schedule of an "average week". How much time do you spend at work, sleep, preparation, with your spouse, with your children, in Bible study and prayer, doing chores around the house, watching TV, doing hobbies, etc.?

_____

_____

_____

_____

	MORNING	AFTERNOON	EVENING
SUN.			
MON.			
TUES.			
WED.			
THURS.			
FRI.			
SAT.			

b) How much time do you spend each week giving undistracted attention to your children?

_____

_____

_____

_____

c) Do you need to change your schedule to spend more time with them? What specific changes will you make?

_____

_____

_____

_____

8. What actions will you take to model the character of God to your children? How will you express:

    •a meaningful touch

    •a spoken message

    •the attachment of high value to the one being blessed

    •the picturing of a special future for the one being blessed

    •an active commitment to fulfill the blessing

9. Look at the following list of family traditions. What do your children enjoy doing? What can you do together? What traditions do you already have? What traditions will you begin?

TRADITIONS [1]

Christmas:

Birthday Box for Baby Jesus
> Make this the most beautiful present under the tree. Have a Bible in the box with the Christmas story marked. Open this present first, and begin gift-giving time by reading the Christmas story.

Decorate Your Children's Doors
> Put wrapping paper and a big bow on each door. Then place a gift tag on it that says something like this: "Meagan, you are God's gift to our family, and God's gift to you is Jesus."

Give Coupons to Family Members
> These are gifts of time and can be special ways to tell others how much we love them.

Valentine's Day:

Baked Valentines
> Bake a cake in a heart-shaped pan. Write Bible verses that deal with love on small strips of paper. Fold them up and wrap them in a small square of foil. Place as many verses as you would like in the batter before baking. After serving the cake, let whoever finds the pieces of foil open them up and read the verses to the group.

Valentine's Day Dinner
> Have a candlelight dinner for your children. You can also choose a specific country for the theme of this special time together. Serve the appropriate ethnic food. Talk about God's love and how we need to take His love to the world. Pray together, giving everyone a specific prayer request for that country.

Easter:

Celebrate with a Romanian Custom

In Romania, an Easter tradition for Christians is to place red eggs on the dinner table (one in front of each person). Before the meal, each person picks up his egg and the head of the table starts by turning to the person on his right and saying, "He is risen." That person responds by saying "He is risen, indeed," and then turns to the person on his right and repeats the process until you have gone around the whole table.

Passover Meal

You can obtain information on this from the book, *Hebrew Christian Passover Haggadah*, by Arnold G. Frucktenbrus, c/o Beth Bar Shalom Fellowship, 460 Sylvan Avenue, P.O. Box 1331, Englewood Cliff, New Jersey 07632.

Birthdays:

VIP Chair

Decorate a special chair for the birthday person. If it is for your child, tell the story of his/her birth and how much he/she was wanted.

Celebrate "Spiritual Birthdays"

For children, give Christian books, tapes, games, etc.

Thanksgiving:

Talk about the people you are especially thankful for. Write them a letter and express your feelings for them.

Read the story of the "Ten Lepers" at your Thanksgiving meal. Jesus healed ten of them and only one came back to thank Him. Talk about the lack of thankfulness.

Weekly:

Have a special breakfast on Saturday mornings: chocolate chip pancakes, waffles, etc.
Schedule family fun night with games and snacks.
Have a family picnic on Sunday afternoon that includes reading and games.

Daily:

Read together before bedtime.
Conduct family devotions in the morning or evening.
Keep a chart of responsibilities for each person (based on their age and ability) with treats for jobs well done.

Other:

Canoeing, hiking, rafting, fishing
Working on hobbies together, building things together
Saving children's clothes or other heirlooms
Special celebrations of birthdays

[1]"Traditions" courtesy of Renée McIntosh.

BREAKING THE CYCLE:

Responding To Your Parents

This step is designed to help you respond to your parents in a way that honors the Lord and reflects His wisdom, love, and power.

1. To summarize the first several steps in this workbook, describe your relationship with your parents when you were a child. How did they show affection? How did they discipline you? Did you feel loved and accepted? Why or why not?

_____

_____

_____

_____

2. What does it mean to honor your parents? (Eph. 6:2-3)

_____

_____

_____

_____

3. Do you feel responsible for making your parents happy? Why or why not?

_____

_____

_____

_____

4. **Principle 1:** See yourself as a conqueror, not a victim.
Read Rom. 8:35, 37. Do you see yourself as a conqueror or as a victim in your relationship with your parents?

_____

_____

_____

_____

5. What differences would it make if you saw yourself as a conqueror?

_____

_____

_____

_____

6. **Principle 2:** See your parents as people, not as villains.
    a) Describe your father's relationship with his parents:

_____

_____

_____

_____

    b) Describe your mother's relationship with her parents:

_____

_____

_____

_____

    c) How does understanding your parents' families affect your attitude toward them?

_____

_____

_____

_____

7. **Principle 3:** Develop a healthy sense of independence.
What does it mean to have a "healthy independence" or objectivity in your relationship with your parents? How would this help you?

_____

_____

_____

_____

8. **Principle 4:** Make godly choices.
Paraphrase these passages:

1 John 4:9-11
By this the love of God was manifested in us, that God has sent His only begotten Son into the world so that we might live through Him. In this is love, not that we loved God, but that He loved us and sent His Son to be the propitiation for our sins. Beloved, if God so loved us, we also ought to love one another.

Paraphrase:

_____

_____

_____

_____

Col. 3:13
...bearing with one another, and forgiving each other, whoever has a complaint against anyone; just as the Lord forgave you, so also should you.

Paraphrase:

_____

_____

_____

_____

Rom. 15:7
Wherefore, accept one another, just as Christ also accepted us to the glory of God.

Paraphrase:

_____
_____
_____
_____

9. List some ways you can communicate God's love, forgiveness and acceptance to your parents.

_____
_____
_____
_____
_____
_____
_____
_____

10. **Principle 5:** Be prepared.
    a) What do you need to do to be prepared in your communications and interactions with your parents?

_____
_____
_____
_____

    b) What should you always do?

_____
_____
_____
_____

c) What should you never do?

_____

_____

_____

_____

d) What is wise to avoid?

_____

_____

_____

_____

e) What is some common ground on which to build the relationship?

_____

_____

_____

_____

CHARACTERISTICS OF CHRIST
AND OUR RELATIONSHIP WITH HIM

How can a person know what God is like? How can a person begin to understand the immensity of the Lord's love, forgiveness, and power so that he can actually experience God's grace, direction, and supernatural strength? By understanding and applying the truths of God's Word!

The Scriptures are our guide. They communicate clearly and powerfully mankind's predicament and the Lord's solution. Each of us needs to develop strong biblical conviction about God's character so that we base our attitudes and actions on His constant love and power, instead of the often fickle nature of others.

This study is designed to help you develop those biblical convictions. To help you think through each passage and consider what it means, we want you to paraphrase the passages in the space provided. Remember the goal is not to "fill in the blanks," but to reflect on the powerful truth of God's Word. That takes time. Be thorough with this exercise. You may want to complete one characteristic per day until you finish the study. That will give you more time to think both about the meaning of each passage and how you can apply it in your daily experience.

Here are eight characteristics of Christ and how we relate to Him. Take plenty of time to reflect on these passages as you paraphrase them.

1. Unconditional love
Because of sin, mankind deserves the righteous wrath of God.

Rom. 2:4-5
Or do you think lightly of the riches of His kindness and forbearance and patience, not knowing that the kindness of God leads you to

repentance? But because of your stubbornness and unrepentant heart you are storing up wrath for yourself in the day of wrath and revelation of the righteous judgment of God....

Paraphrase:

_____

_____

_____

_____

Eph. 2:1-3
And you were dead in your trespasses and sins, in which you formerly walked according to the course of this world, according to the prince of the power of the air, of the spirit that is now working in the sons of disobedience. Among them we too all formerly lived in the lusts of our flesh, indulging the desires of the flesh and of the mind, and were by nature children of wrath, even as the rest.

Paraphrase:

_____

_____

_____

_____

But Christ's death averted that wrath for us. Therefore, we are deeply loved by God.

1 John 4:9-10
By this the love of God was manifested in us, that God has sent His only begotten Son into the world so that we might live through Him. In this is love, not that we loved God, but that He loved us and sent His Son to be the propitiation for our sins.

Paraphrase:

_____

_____

_____

John 3:16-18

For God so loved the world, that He gave His only begotten Son, that whoever believes in Him should not perish, but have eternal life. For God did not send the Son into the world to judge the world, but that the world should be saved through Him. He who believes in Him is not judged; he who does not believe has been judged already, because he has not believed in the name of the only begotten Son of God.

Paraphrase:

_____

_____

_____

_____

Eph. 2:4-9

But God, being rich in mercy, because of His great love with which He loved us, even when we were dead in our transgressions, made us alive together with Christ (by grace you have been saved), and raised us up with Him, and seated us with Him in the heavenly places, in Christ Jesus, in order that in the ages to come He might show the surpassing riches of His grace in kindness toward us in Christ Jesus. For by grace you have been saved through faith; and that not of yourselves, it is the gift of God; not as a result of works, that no one should boast.

Paraphrase:

_____

_____

_____

II Thess. 2:16-17
Now may our Lord Jesus Christ Himself and God our Father, who has loved us and given us eternal comfort and good hope by grace, comfort and strengthen your hearts in every good work and word.

Paraphrase:

_____

_____

_____

_____

Rom. 8:38-39
For I am convinced that neither death, nor life, nor angels, nor principalities, nor things present, nor things to come, nor powers, nor height, nor depth, nor any other created thing, shall be able to separate us from the love of God, which is in Christ Jesus our Lord.

Paraphrase:

_____

_____

_____

_____

As we grasp the truth of God's unconditional love, we are able to love others unconditionally.

2. Complete forgiveness
Our sins separated us from God.

Rom. 3:9-20
What then? Are we better than they? Not at all; for we have already charged that both Jews and Greeks are all under sin; as it is written, "There is none righteous, not even one; there is none who understands, there is none who seeks for God; all have turned aside, together they have become useless; there is none who does

good, there is not even one." "Their throat is an open grave, with their tongues they keep deceiving," "The poison of asps is under their lips"; "Whose mouth is full of cursing and bitterness"; "Their feet are swift to shed blood, destruction and misery are in their paths, and the path of peace have they not known." "There is no fear of God before their eyes." Now we know that whatever the Law says, it speaks to those who are under the Law, that every mouth may be closed, and all the world may become accountable to God: because by the works of the Law no flesh will be justified in His sight; for through the Law comes the knowledge of sin.

Paraphrase:

_____
_____
_____
_____

But Christ's death completely paid our debt of sin so that we are completely forgiven.

Col. 2:13-14
And when you were dead in your transgressions and the uncircumcision of your flesh, He made you alive together with Him, having forgiven us all our transgressions, having canceled out the certificate of debt consisting of decrees against us and which was hostile to us; and He has taken it out of the way, having nailed it to the cross.

Paraphrase:

_____
_____
_____
_____

Rom. 5:6-11
For while we were still helpless, at the right time Christ died for the
ungodly. For one will hardly die for a righteous man; though
perhaps for the good man someone would dare even to die. But God
demonstrates His own love toward us, in that while we were yet
sinners, Christ died for us. Much more then, having now been
justified by His blood, we shall be saved from the wrath of God
through Him. For if while we were enemies, we were reconciled to
God through the death of His Son, much more, having been
reconciled, we shall be saved by His life. And not only this, but we
also exult in God through our Lord Jesus Christ, through whom we
have now received the reconciliation.

Paraphrase:

_____

_____

_____

_____

Eph. 1:7
In Him we have redemption through His blood, the forgiveness of our
trespasses, according to the riches of His grace....

Paraphrase:

_____

_____

_____

_____

Eph. 2:1-10
And you were dead in your trespasses and sins, in which you
formerly walked according to the course of this world, according
to the prince of the power of the air, of the spirit that is now
working in the sons of disobedience. Among them we too all
formerly lived in the lusts of our flesh, indulging the desires of the

flesh and of the mind, and were by nature chlidren of wrath, even as the rest. But God, being rich in mercy, because of His great love with which He loved us, even when we were dead in our transgressions, made us alive together with Christ (by grace you have been saved), and raised us up with Him, and seated us with Him in the heavenly places, in Christ Jesus, in order that in the ages to come He might show the surpassing riches of His grace in kindness toward us in Christ Jesus. For by grace you have been saved through faith; and that not of yourselves, it is the gift of God; not as a result of works, that no one should boast. For we are His workmanship, created in Christ Jesus for good works, which God prepared beforehand, that we should walk in them.

Paraphrase:

_____

_____

_____

_____

Rom. 3:23-24
...for all have sinned and fall short of the glory of God, being justified as a gift by His grace through the redemption which is in Christ Jesus....

Paraphrase:

_____

_____

_____

Rom. 4:4-5
Now to the one who works, his wage is not reckoned as a favor, but as what is due. But to the one who does not work, but believes in Him who justifies the ungodly, his faith is reckoned as righteousness....

Paraphrase:

_____

_____

_____

_____

Because we are forgiven by God, we can forgive others.

Col. 3:13

...bearing with one another, and forgiving each other, whoever has a complaint against anyone; just as the Lord forgave you, so also should you.

Paraphrase:

_____

_____

_____

_____

Matt. 18:21-35

Then Peter came and said to Him, "Lord, how often shall my brother sin against me and I forgive him? Up to seven times?" Jesus said to him, "I do not say to you, up to seven times, but up to seventy times seven. For this reason the kingdom of heaven may be compared to a certain king who wished to settle accounts with his slaves. And when he had begun to settle them, there was brought to him one who owed him ten thousand talents. But since he did not have the means to repay, his lord commanded him to be sold, along with his wife and children and all that he had, and repayment to be made. The slave therefore falling down, prostrated himself before him, saying, 'Have patience with me, and I will repay you everything.' And the lord of that slave felt compassion and released him and forgave him the debt. But that slave went out and found one of his fellow slaves who owed him a hundred denarii; and he seized him and began to choke him, saying, 'Pay back what you owe.' So his fellow slave fell down and began to entreat him, saying, 'Have patience with me and I will repay you.' He was unwilling however, but went and threw him in prison until he should pay back what was owed. So when his fellow slaves saw what had happened, they were deeply grieved and came and reported to their lord all that had happened. Then summoning him, his lord said to him, 'You wicked slave, I forgave you all that debt because you entreated me. Should you not also have had mercy on your fellow slave, even as I had mercy on you?' And his lord, moved with anger, handed him over to the torturers until he should repay all that was owed him. So shall My heavenly Father also do to you, if each of you does not forgive his brother from your heart."

Paraphrase:

_____

_____

_____

_____

_____

_____

_____

_____

3. Total acceptance

Because of our sins, we were enemies of God.

Rom. 5:10

For if while we were enemies, we were reconciled to God through the death of His Son, much more, having been reconciled, we shall be saved by His life.

Paraphrase:

_____

_____

_____

Christ's payment for our sins took away the barrier between us and Him so that we are now His beloved children and His beloved friends.

Rom. 8:15-17
For you have not received a spirit of slavery leading to fear again, but you have received a spirit of adoption as sons by which we cry out, "Abba! Father!" The Spirit Himself bears witness with our spirit that we are children of God, and if children, heirs also, heirs of God and fellow heirs with Christ, if indeed we suffer with Him in order that we may also be glorified with Him.

Paraphrase:

_____

_____

_____

_____

Gal. 4:5-7
...in order that He might redeem those who were under the Law, that we might receive the adoption as sons. And because you are sons, God has sent forth the Spirit of His Son into our hearts, crying, "Abba! Father!" Therefore you are no longer a slave, but a son; and if a son, then an heir through God.

Paraphrase:

_____

_____

_____

_____

Col. 1:19-22
For it was the Father's good pleasure for all the fulness to dwell in Him, and through Him to reconcile all things to Himself, having made peace through the blood of His cross; through Him, I say, whether things on earth or things in heaven. And although you

*were formerly alienated and hostile in mind, engaged in evil deeds,
yet He has now reconciled you in His fleshly body through death,
in order to present you before Him holy and blameless and beyond
reproach....*

Paraphrase:

_____

_____

_____

John 17:23-24

*"...I in them, and Thou in Me, that they may be perfected in unity,
that the world may know that Thou didst send Me, and didst love
them, even as Thou didst love Me. Father, I desire that they also,
whom Thou hast given Me, be with Me where I am, in order that
they may behold My glory, which Thou hast given Me; for Thou
didst love Me before the foundation of the world."*

Paraphrase:

_____

_____

_____

_____

John 20:17

*Jesus said to her, "Stop clinging to Me, for I have not yet ascended
to the Father; but go to My brethren, and say to them, 'I ascend to
My Father and your Father, and My God and your God.'"*

Paraphrase:

_____

_____

_____

_____

Because we are totally accepted by God, we can unconditionally accept others.

> Rom. 15:7
> *Wherefore, accept one another, just as Christ also accepted us to the glory of God.*

Paraphrase:

_____

_____

_____

_____

4. Authority and power

Christ has infinite authority and power.

> Col. 2:15
> *When He had disarmed the rulers and authorities, He made a public display of them, having triumphed over them through Him.*

Paraphrase:

_____

_____

_____

_____

> Eph. 1:18-22
> *I pray that the eyes of your heart may be enlightened, so that you may know what is the hope of His calling, what are the riches of the glory of His inheritance in the saints, and what is the surpassing greatness of His power toward us who believe. These are in accordance with the working of the strength of His might which He brought about in Christ, when He raised Him from the dead, and seated Him at His right hand in the heavenly places, far above all rule and authority and power and dominion, and every*

name that is named, not only in this age, but also in the one to come. And He put all things in subjection under His feet, and gave Him as head over all things to the church....

Paraphrase:

_____

_____

_____

_____

I Cor. 3:6-7

I planted, Apollos watered, but God was causing the growth. So then neither the one who plants nor the one who waters is anything, but God who causes the growth.

Paraphrase:

_____

_____

_____

_____

II Cor. 3:4-6

And such confidence we have through Christ toward God. Not that we are adequate in ourselves to consider anything as coming from ourselves, but our adequacy is from God, who also made us adequate as servants of a new covenant, not of the letter, but of the Spirit; for the letter kills, but the Spirit gives life.

Paraphrase:

_____

_____

_____

_____

Eph. 6:10-20

Finally, be strong in the Lord, and in the strength of His might. Put on the full armor of God, that you may be able to stand firm against the schemes of the devil. For our struggle is not against flesh and blood, but against the rulers, against the powers, against the world forces of this darkness, against the spiritual forces of wickedness in the heavenly places. Therefore, take up the full armor of God, that you may be able to resist in the evil day, and having done everything, to stand firm. Stand firm therefore, "having girded your loins with truth," and "having put on the breastplate of righteousness," and having shod "your feet with the preparation of the gospel of peace;" in addition to all, taking up the shield of faith with which you will be able to extinguish all the flaming missiles of the evil one. And take "the helmet of salvation," and the sword of the Spirit, which is the word of God. With all prayer and petition pray at all times in the Spirit, and with this in view, be on the alert with all perseverance and petition for all the saints, and pray on my behalf, that utterance may be given to me in the opening of my mouth, to make known with boldness the mystery of the gospel, for which I am an ambassador in chains; that in proclaiming it I may speak boldly, as I ought to speak.

Paraphrase:

_____

_____

_____

_____

5. Hope

There is no hope apart from Christ.

Eph. 2:12

...remember that you were at that time separate from Christ, excluded from the commonwealth of Israel, and strangers to

the covenants of promise, having no hope and without God in
the world.

Paraphrase:

_____

_____

_____

_____

But His love, forgiveness, and power gives us hope.

Heb. 6:19
*This hope we have as an anchor of the soul, a hope both sure and
steadfast and one which enters within the veil....*

Paraphrase:

_____

_____

_____

_____

I Pet. 1:3
*Blessed be the God and Father of our Lord Jesus Christ, who
according to His great mercy has caused us to be born again to a
living hope through the resurrection of Jesus Christ from the
dead....*

Paraphrase:

_____

_____

_____

_____

Titus 3:7
...that being justified by His grace we might be made heirs according to the hope of eternal life.

Paraphrase:

_____

_____

_____

_____

Rom. 5:3-5
And not only this, but we also exult in our tribulations, knowing that tribulation brings about perseverance; and perseverance, proven character; and proven character, hope; and hope does not disappoint, because the love of God has been poured out within our hearts through the Holy Spirit who was given to us.

Paraphrase:

_____

_____

_____

_____

Rom. 8:28
And we know that God causes all things to work together for good to those who love God, to those who are called according to His purpose.

Paraphrase:

_____

_____

_____

_____

6. Faithfulness

Christ is always faithful to be Himself and to do what He has promised.

> I Cor. 10:13
> *No temptation has overtaken you but such as is common to man; and God is faithful, who will not allow you to be tempted beyond what you are able, but with the temptation will provide the way of escape also, that you may be able to endure it.*

Paraphrase:

_____

_____

_____

_____

> I Thess. 5:24
> *Faithful is He who calls you, and He also will bring it to pass.*

Paraphrase:

_____

_____

_____

_____

> Heb. 10:23
> *Let us hold fast the confession of our hope without wavering, for He who promised is faithful....*

Paraphrase:

_____

_____

_____

_____

Matt. 23:23
Woe to you, scribes and Pharisees, hypocrites! For you tithe mint and dill and cummin, and have neglected the weightier provisions of the law: justice and mercy and faithfulness; but these are the things you should have done without neglecting the others.

Paraphrase:

_____

_____
_____

II Tim. 2:11-13
It is a trustworthy statement: For if we died with Him, we shall also live with Him; If we endure, we shall also reign with Him; If we deny Him, He also will deny us; If we are faithless, He remains faithful; for He cannot deny Himself.

Paraphrase:

_____

_____
_____
_____

7. Wisdom

The Lord has all knowledge and all wisdom. He knows what is best for us, and He will give us wisdom to know how we can honor Him in every situation.

James 1:5-6
But if any of you lacks wisdom, let him ask of God, who gives to all men generously and without reproach, and it will be given to him. But let him ask in faith without any doubting, for the one who doubts is like the surf of the sea driven and tossed by the wind.

Paraphrase:

_____

_____

_____

_____

Matt. 11:19

The Son of Man came eating and drinking, and they say, "Behold, a gluttonous man and a drunkard, a friend of tax-gatherers and sinners!" Yet wisdom is vindicated by her deeds.

Paraphrase:

_____

_____

_____

_____

I Cor. 2:1-5

And when I came to you, brethren, I did not come with superiority of speech or of wisdom, proclaiming to you the testimony of God. For I determined to know nothing among you except Jesus Christ, and Him crucified. And I was with you in weakness and in fear and in much trembling. And my message and my preaching were not in persuasive words of wisdom, but in demonstration of the Spirit and of power, that your faith should not rest on the wisdom of men, but on the power of God.

Paraphrase:

_____

_____

_____

II Cor. 1:12

For our proud confidence is this, the testimony of our conscience, that in holiness and godly sincerity, not in fleshly wisdom but in the grace of God, we have conducted ourselves in the world, and especially toward you.

Paraphrase:

_____

_____

_____

_____

Eph. 5:15-21
Therefore be careful how you walk, not as unwise men, but as wise, making the most of your time, because the days are evil. So then do not be foolish, but understand what the will of the Lord is. And do not get drunk with wine, for that is dissipation, but be filled with the Spirit, speaking to one another in psalms and hymns and spiritual songs, singing and making melody with your heart to the Lord; always giving thanks for all things in the name of our Lord Jesus Christ to God, even the Father; and be subject to one another in the fear of Christ.

Paraphrase:

_____

_____

_____

_____

8. Purpose

Christ's purpose was to honor the Father by accurately representing Him on earth. It is our privilege and calling to know Him, love Him, and serve Him as His ambassadors.

Matt. 22:34-40
But when the Pharisees heard that He had put the Sadducees to silence, they gathered themselves together. And one of them, a lawyer, asked Him a question, testing Him, "Teacher, which is the

great commandment in the Law?" And He said to him, "'You shall love the Lord your God with all your heart, and with all your soul, and with all your mind.' This is the great and foremost commandment. And a second is like it, 'You shall love your neighbor as yourself.' On these two commandments depend the whole Law and the Prophets."

Paraphrase:

_____

_____

_____

_____

Phil. 3:7-10
But whatever things were gain to me, those things I have counted as loss for the sake of Christ. More than that, I count all things to be loss in view of the surpassing value of knowing Christ Jesus my Lord, for whom I have suffered the loss of all things, and count them but rubbish in order that I may gain Christ, and may be found in Him, not having a righteousness of my own derived from the Law, but that which is through faith in Christ, the righteousness which comes from God on the basis of faith, that I may know Him, and the power of His resurrection and the fellowship of His sufferings, being conformed to His death....

Paraphrase:

_____

_____

_____

_____

II Cor. 5:18-21
Now all these things are from God, who reconciled us to Himself through Christ, and gave us the ministry of reconciliation, namely, that God was in Christ reconciling the world to Himself, not

counting their trespasses against them, and He has committed to us the word of reconciliation. Therefore, we are ambassadors for Christ, as though God were entreating through us; we beg you on behalf of Christ, be reconciled to God. He made Him who knew no sin to be sin on our behalf, that we might become the righteousness of God in Him.

Paraphrase:

_____

_____

_____

_____

II Cor. 5:14-15
For the love of Christ controls us, having concluded this, that one died for all, therefore all died; and He died for all, that they who live should no longer live for themselves, but for Him who died and rose again on their behalf.

Paraphrase:

_____

_____

_____

_____

II Cor. 5:9
Therefore also we have as our ambition, whether at home or absent, to be pleasing to Him.

Paraphrase:

_____

_____

_____

_____

Eph. 2:10
*For we are His workmanship, created in Christ Jesus for good
works, which God prepared beforehand, that we should walk in
them.*

Paraphrase:

_____

_____

_____

_____

Matt. 28:18-20
*And Jesus came up and spoke to them, saying, "All authority has
been given to Me in heaven and on earth. Go therefore and make
disciples of all the nations, baptizing them in the name of the
Father and the Son and the Holy Spirit, teaching them to observe
all that I commanded you; and lo, I am with you always, even to
the end of the age."*

Paraphrase:

_____

_____

_____

_____

Which passage in each section has been most meaningful to you?
List the passage and describe why it is so meaningful. Also, describe how
you can apply the truth of that passage in your life.

1. Unconditional love

_____

_____

_____

_____

_____

_____

_____

2. Complete forgiveness

_____

_____

_____

_____

_____

_____

_____

3. Total acceptance

_____

_____

_____

_____

_____

_____

_____

4. Authority and power

_____

_____

_____

_____

_____

_____

_____

5. Hope

_____

_____

_____

_____

_____

_____

_____

_____

_____

_____

6. Faithfulness

_____

_____

_____

_____

_____

_____

_____

_____

7. Wisdom

_____

_____

_____

_____

_____

_____

_____

8. Purpose

_____

_____

_____

_____

_____

_____

_____

_____

_____

STEP FOURTEEN

CHRIST REPAIRS
DAMAGED LIVES

Here is a plan you can use for the rest of your life. It will help you use problems as the way to develop a deeper and richer relationship with God the Father through His Son.

1. Before you continue, review Chapter Ten.

Step Fourteen is built on the foundational truths explained in detail in Chapter Ten. *Reread the chapter before continuing with this section.*

2. Return to Step Five, select a characteristic you recognized in one of your parents which is now a characteristic of your life.

In the space below, briefly describe this characteristic:

_____

_____

_____

_____

This particular characteristic probably carries with it a sense of pain for you. It has probably caused you a lot of concern in the past.

a) Describe how you have responded to this characteristic in your parents.

_____

_____

_____

b) How have you *felt* about this characteristic in yourself?

_____

_____

_____

_____

_____

c) How have you *acted*?

_____

_____

_____

_____

Behind your response is one of Satan's lies. Which one listed below does your response relate to?

Check the appropriate box or boxes:

❏ **The Fear Of Failure:** *I must meet certain standards in order to feel good about myself.*

❏ **The Fear Of Rejection:** *I must be approved by certain others to feel good about myself.*

❏ **The Fear Of Being Punished:** *Those who fail (including myself) are unworthy of love and deserve to be punished.*

❏ **The Feeling Of Shame:** *I am what I am. I cannot change. I am hopeless.*

3. Use the truth of God's Word to confront these lies.

In the preceding Step, there is a list of eight characteristics of Christ. With each one, there are Scriptures which describe these characteristics for you. These Scriptures reveal the character of your Heavenly Father as demonstrated by the life and words of Jesus.

In the last exercise, you selected a worry or fear you experience because of negative parental influences. Now, look through these characteristics until you find the one which best relates to your fear or fears.

a) In the space below, write the characteristic of Christ you have selected:

_____

_____

_____

b) Look up the Scriptures mentioned. Underline the ones in your Bible which you want to remember. (You may even decide to memorize some of them!)

c) Which particular verse (or verses) pertaining to this characteristic of Christ is most meaningful to you? Write it out here.

_____

_____

_____

_____

_____

_____

_____

_____

d) Meditate on these verses. What do they teach you about your worth and about your ability to overcome your fear?

_____

_____

_____

_____

_____

_____

_____

4. Express yourself to the Lord, *realizing* your situation, *rejecting* the lies you may be believing and *replacing* those lies with the powerful truth of God's Word.

You may want to include some of these thoughts in your prayers:

Realize
Father, I need Your help. I feel angry (or hurt or...) because ....
("Pour out your heart to the Lord." Ps. 62:8)

Reject
Lord, I am experiencing the fear of rejection (or failure, or...)

Replace
Father, thank You for the truth of Your Word." (Select a passage from the preceding Step that confronts the lie. Think and pray about how you can apply the truth of God's Word to your situation.)
Father, I claim Your peace and protection. You alone are my Provider. You totally understand me, and You care about me. Thank You that, because of Christ's death to pay for my sins, I am deeply loved, completely forgiven, fully pleasing, and totally accepted by You.
Those times that I thought You were distant and insensitive, I was deceived. There is not one moment that You are not sensitive to every detail of my life.
Recall some times that you felt understood and comforted by the Lord:

_____

_____

_____

_____

_____

_____

_____

_____

_____

_____

_____

Thank you, Lord, that You understand, You care, and You provide for me. Your truth and Your Spirit are stronger than anything that can come into my life.

Sometimes our hurt and pain is changed to joy rather quickly as we reflect on the character of God. At other times, however, our feelings don't change so rapidly. Don't despair. Emotions are fickle. Continue to concentrate on the truth of God's Word, and put yourself in an environment where you can experience the love and acceptance of God and see His character modeled by mature, honest believers. Growth takes time *and* fertile soil.

5. Begin a twenty-day experiment with this pattern .

Take time each day for the next twenty days to discover the true nature of your Heavenly Father by sharing your stresses with Him. (You will find forms to help you with this at the end of this workbook.) You may wish to return to Step Five, choosing additional symptoms from those you checked. Or, like Ronald, you may face some difficult problems in current situations.

In either case, refer daily to the list of "Characteristics of Christ." As the twenty days pass, you will begin to experience the positive result of confronting every negative thought with the loving and powerful character of God.

As you mature, your confidence in Him will give you a new way of dealing with stress. You will no longer be controlled by circumstances. Instead, you will be controlled by the Holy Spirit of God, and you will begin to discover the joy that comes from His control.

STEP FIFTEEN

TWENTY DAYS TO
VICTORIOUS LIVING

For the next twenty days, select a specific place and time to complete Step Fifteen. Develop a habit in your scheduled activities which could permanently change your life.

Everything else of value in your life happens by being scheduled, doesn't it? You have a regular time to eat, to begin the workday, to rest, to watch television. Schedule a set time to reflect on the character of God. This workbook provides blank forms for you to use for the next twenty days. They will repeat the pattern that you were introduced to in Chapter Ten and Step Five.

Use the list of "Characteristics of Christ" daily. Each time you catch yourself feeling anxious because of a situation, a comment, a thought, a problem, or a relationship, take that condition to your meeting place. As the twenty days pass, you will expose many negative thoughts to the character of God.

Twenty days from now, you will have a new pattern for living—one which we trust you will continue indefinitely.

Realize
1. Be objective about your stressful situation by writing it out.

Reject
2. Next, list the fear, or fears, triggered by it.

Replace
3. Review the "Characteristics of Christ" and select one appropriate to your situation.

4. Write out the Scriptures which describe this characteristic.
5. In prayer, affirm the application to your situation.
6. Recall other times when the Father has understood you completely, and include thanksgiving for them.
7. Remember other occasions when you were deceived into believing that God didn't understand you.
8. Confess those times as wrong; praise the Lord for His present understanding and the victory He is now giving you.

DAY ONE

Date:__/__/__

1. *Realize*
    Describe your situation:

    _____

    _____

    _____

    _____

    _____

    _____

2. *Reject*
    Which of the four fears does this trigger for you?

    •**The Fear of Failure:** *I must meet certain standards in order to feel good about myself.*

    •**The Need to be Punished:** *Those who fail (including myself) are unworthy of love and deserve to be punished.*

    •**The Fear of Rejection:** *I must be approved by certain others to feel good about myself.*

    •**The Feeling of Shame:** *I am what I am. I cannot change. I am hopeless.*

3. *Replace*
    a) What characteristic of Christ helps overcome this fear? Write out the Scriptures on a separate sheet.

    _____

    _____

_____

_____

_____

_____

_____

b) How can you apply this perfect characteristic to this particular problem?

_____

_____

_____

_____

_____

_____

c) List one or more times when the Lord has understood you completely when you faced this problem:

_____

_____

_____

_____

_____

_____

d) List occasions when you were deceived, believing that God didn't understand you when you faced this problem:

_____

_____

_____

_____

_____

_____

e) Confess (agree) that your perception of Him was wrong when you were deceived, and then praise Him for understanding you and for giving you love, forgiveness, and power.

_____

_____

_____

_____

_____

_____

_____

DAY TWO

Date:__/__/__

1. *Realize*
Describe your situation:

_____

_____

_____

_____

_____

_____

_____

2. *Reject*
Which of the four fears does this trigger for you?

•**The Fear of Failure:** *I must meet certain standards in order to feel good about myself.*

•**The Need to be Punished:** *Those who fail (including myself) are unworthy of love and deserve to be punished.*

•**The Fear of Rejection:** *I must be approved by certain others to feel good about myself.*

•**The Feeling of Shame:** *I am what I am. I cannot change. I am hopeless.*

3. *Replace*
a) What characteristic of Christ helps overcome this fear? Write out the Scriptures on a separate sheet.

_____

_____

_____

_____

_____

_____

_____

b) How can you apply this perfect characteristic to this particular problem?

_____

_____

_____

_____

_____

_____

c) List one or more times when the Lord has understood you completely when you faced this problem:

_____

_____

_____

_____

_____

_____

d) List occasions when you were deceived, believing that God didn't understand you when you faced this problem:

_____

_____

_____

_____

_____

_____

e) Confess (agree) that your perception of Him was wrong when you were deceived, and then praise Him for understanding you and for giving you love, forgiveness, and power.

DAY THREE

Date:__/__/__

1. *Realize*
Describe your situation:

_____

_____

_____

_____

_____

_____

_____

2. *Reject*
Which of the four fears does this trigger for you?

• **The Fear of Failure:** *I must meet certain standards in order to feel good about myself.*

• **The Need to be Punished:** *Those who fail (including myself) are unworthy of love and deserve to be punished.*

• **The Fear of Rejection:** *I must be approved by certain others to feel good about myself.*

• **The Feeling of Shame:** *I am what I am. I cannot change. I am hopeless.*

3. *Replace*
a) What characteristic of Christ helps overcome this fear? Write out the Scriptures on a separate sheet.

_____

_____

_____

_____

_____

_____

_____

_____

b) How can you apply this perfect characteristic to this particular problem?

_____

_____

_____

_____

_____

_____

c) List one or more times when the Lord has understood you completely when you faced this problem:

_____

_____

_____

_____

_____

_____

d) List occasions when you were deceived, believing that God didn't understand you when you faced this problem:

_____

_____

_____

_____

_____

_____

e) Confess (agree) that your perception of Him was wrong when you were deceived, and then praise Him for understanding you and for giving you love, forgiveness, and power.

_____

_____

_____

_____

_____

_____

_____

DAY FOUR

Date:___/___/___

1. *Realize*
   Describe your situation:

   _____
   _____
   _____
   _____
   _____
   _____
   _____

2. *Reject*
   Which of the four fears does this trigger for you?

   •**The Fear of Failure:** *I must meet certain standards in order to feel good about myself.*

   •**The Need to be Punished:** *Those who fail (including myself) are unworthy of love and deserve to be punished.*

   •**The Fear of Rejection:** *I must be approved by certain others to feel good about myself.*

   •**The Feeling of Shame:** *I am what I am. I cannot change. I am hopeless.*

3. *Replace*
   a) What characteristic of Christ helps overcome this fear? Write out the Scriptures on a separate sheet.

   _____
   _____

_____
_____
_____
_____
_____

b) How can you apply this perfect characteristic to this particular problem?

_____
_____
_____
_____
_____
_____
_____

c) List one or more times when the Lord has understood you completely when you faced this problem:

_____
_____
_____
_____
_____
_____
_____

d) List occasions when you were deceived, believing that God didn't understand you when you faced this problem:

_____
_____
_____
_____
_____
_____

e) Confess (agree) that your perception of Him was wrong when you were deceived, and then praise Him for understanding you and for giving you love, forgiveness, and power.

_____

_____

_____

_____

_____

_____

_____

DAY FIVE

Date:___/___/___

1.   *Realize*
Describe your situation:

_____

_____

_____

_____

_____

_____

_____

2.   *Reject*
Which of the four fears does this trigger for you?

• **The Fear of Failure:** *I must meet certain standards in order to feel good about myself.*

• **The Need to be Punished:** *Those who fail (including myself) are unworthy of love and deserve to be punished.*

• **The Fear of Rejection:** *I must be approved by certain others to feel good about myself.*

• **The Feeling of Shame:** *I am what I am. I cannot change. I am hopeless.*

3.   *Replace*
a) What characteristic of Christ helps overcome this fear? Write out the Scriptures on a separate sheet.

_____

_____

_____
_____
_____
_____
_____

b) How can you apply this perfect characteristic to this particular problem?

_____
_____
_____
_____
_____
_____

c) List one or more times when the Lord has understood you completely when you faced this problem:

_____
_____
_____
_____
_____
_____

d) List occasions when you were deceived, believing that God didn't understand you when you faced this problem:

_____
_____
_____
_____
_____
_____

e) Confess (agree) that your perception of Him was wrong when you were deceived, and then praise Him for understanding you and for giving you love, forgiveness, and power.

DAY SIX

Date:__/__/__

1. *Realize*
Describe your situation:

_____

_____

_____

_____

_____

_____

_____

2. *Reject*
Which of the four fears does this trigger for you?

•**The Fear of Failure:** *I must meet certain standards in order to feel good about myself.*

•**The Need to be Punished:** *Those who fail (including myself) are unworthy of love and deserve to be punished.*

•**The Fear of Rejection:** *I must be approved by certain others to feel good about myself.*

•**The Feeling of Shame:** *I am what I am. I cannot change. I am hopeless.*

3. *Replace*
a) What characteristic of Christ helps overcome this fear? Write out the Scriptures on a separate sheet.

_____

_____

_____
_____
_____
_____
_____

b) How can you apply this perfect characteristic to this particular problem?

_____
_____
_____
_____
_____

c) List one or more times when the Lord has understood you completely when you faced this problem:

_____
_____
_____
_____
_____

d) List occasions when you were deceived, believing that God didn't understand you when you faced this problem:

_____
_____
_____
_____
_____

e) Confess (agree) that your perception of Him was wrong when you were deceived, and then praise Him for understanding you and for giving you love, forgiveness, and power.

_____

_____

_____

_____

_____

_____

_____

DAY SEVEN

Date:__/__/__

1. **Realize**
   Describe your situation:

   _____
   _____
   _____
   _____
   _____
   _____
   _____

2. **Reject**
   Which of the four fears does this trigger for you?

   •**The Fear of Failure:** *I must meet certain standards in order to feel good about myself.*

   •**The Need to be Punished:** *Those who fail (including myself) are unworthy of love and deserve to be punished.*

   •**The Fear of Rejection:** *I must be approved by certain others to feel good about myself.*

   •**The Feeling of Shame:** *I am what I am. I cannot change. I am hopeless.*

3. **Replace**
   a) What characteristic of Christ helps overcome this fear? Write out the Scriptures on a separate sheet.

   _____
   _____

_____

_____

_____

_____

_____

b) How can you apply this perfect characteristic to this particular problem?

_____

_____

_____

_____

_____

_____

c) List one or more times when the Lord has understood you completely when you faced this problem:

_____

_____

_____

_____

_____

_____

d) List occasions when you were deceived, believing that God didn't understand you when you faced this problem:

_____

_____

_____

_____

_____

_____

e) Confess (agree) that your perception of Him was wrong when you were deceived, and then praise Him for understanding you and for giving you love, forgiveness, and power.

_____

_____

_____

_____

_____

_____

_____

DAY EIGHT

Date:__/__/__

1. *Realize*
Describe your situation:

_____

_____

_____

_____

_____

_____

_____

2. *Reject*
Which of the four fears does this trigger for you?

•**The Fear of Failure:** *I must meet certain standards in order to feel good about myself.*

•**The Need to be Punished:** *Those who fail (including myself) are unworthy of love and deserve to be punished.*

•**The Fear of Rejection:** *I must be approved by certain others to feel good about myself.*

•**The Feeling of Shame:** *I am what I am. I cannot change. I am hopeless.*

3. *Replace*
a) What characteristic of Christ helps overcome this fear? Write out the Scriptures on a separate sheet.

_____

_____

_____

_____

_____

_____

_____

b) How can you apply this perfect characteristic to this particular problem?

_____

_____

_____

_____

_____

_____

c) List one or more times when the Lord has understood you completely when you faced this problem:

_____

_____

_____

_____

_____

d) List occasions when you were deceived, believing that God didn't understand you when you faced this problem:

_____

_____

_____

_____

_____

e) Confess (agree) that your perception of Him was wrong when you were deceived, and then praise Him for understanding you and for giving you love, forgiveness, and power.

_____

_____

_____

_____

_____

_____

_____

DAY NINE

Date:__/__/__

1. *Realize*
Describe your situation:

_____

_____

_____

_____

_____

_____

_____

2. *Reject*
Which of the four fears does this trigger for you?

•**The Fear of Failure:** *I must meet certain standards in order to feel good about myself.*

•**The Need to be Punished:** *Those who fail (including myself) are unworthy of love and deserve to be punished.*

•**The Fear of Rejection:** *I must be approved by certain others to feel good about myself.*

•**The Feeling of Shame:** *I am what I am. I cannot change. I am hopeless.*

3. *Replace*
a) What characteristic of Christ helps overcome this fear? Write out the Scriptures on a separate sheet.

_____

_____

_____

_____

_____

_____

_____

b) How can you apply this perfect characteristic to this particular problem?

_____

_____

_____

_____

_____

_____

c) List one or more times when the Lord has understood you completely when you faced this problem:

_____

_____

_____

_____

_____

_____

d) List occasions when you were deceived, believing that God didn't understand you when you faced this problem:

_____

_____

_____

_____

_____

e) Confess (agree) that your perception of Him was wrong when you were deceived, and then praise Him for understanding you and for giving you love, forgiveness, and power.

_____

_____

_____

_____

_____

_____

_____

DAY TEN

Date:__/__/__

1. *Realize*
Describe your situation:

_____

_____

_____

_____

_____

_____

_____

2. *Reject*
Which of the four fears does this trigger for you?

• **The Fear of Failure:** *I must meet certain standards in order to feel good about myself.*

• **The Need to be Punished:** *Those who fail (including myself) are unworthy of love and deserve to be punished.*

• **The Fear of Rejection:** *I must be approved by certain others to feel good about myself.*

• **The Feeling of Shame:** *I am what I am. I cannot change. I am hopeless.*

3. *Replace*
a) What characteristic of Christ helps overcome this fear? Write out the Scriptures on a separate sheet.

_____

_____

_____
_____
_____
_____
_____

b) How can you apply this perfect characteristic to this particular problem?

_____
_____
_____
_____
_____
_____
_____

c) List one or more times when the Lord has understood you completely when you faced this problem:

_____
_____
_____
_____
_____
_____
_____

d) List occasions when you were deceived, believing that God didn't understand you when you faced this problem:

_____
_____
_____
_____
_____
_____

e) Confess (agree) that your perception of Him was wrong when you were deceived, and then praise Him for understanding you and for giving you love, forgiveness, and power.

_____

_____

_____

_____

_____

_____

_____

DAY ELEVEN

Date:___/___/___

1. *Realize*
Describe your situation:

_____

_____

_____

_____

_____

_____

_____

2. *Reject*
Which of the four fears does this trigger for you?

• **The Fear of Failure:** *I must meet certain standards in order to feel good about myself.*

• **The Need to be Punished:** *Those who fail (including myself) are unworthy of love and deserve to be punished.*

• **The Fear of Rejection:** *I must be approved by certain others to feel good about myself.*

• **The Feeling of Shame:** *I am what I am. I cannot change. I am hopeless.*

3. *Replace*
a) What characteristic of Christ helps overcome this fear? Write out the Scriptures on a separate sheet.

_____

_____

_____

_____

_____

_____

_____

b) How can you apply this perfect characteristic to this particular problem?

_____

_____

_____

_____

_____

c) List one or more times when the Lord has understood you completely when you faced this problem:

_____

_____

_____

_____

_____

d) List occasions when you were deceived, believing that God didn't understand you when you faced this problem:

_____

_____

_____

_____

_____

e) Confess (agree) that your perception of Him was wrong when you were deceived, and then praise Him for understanding you and for giving you love, forgiveness, and power.

_____

_____

_____

_____

_____

_____

_____

DAY TWELVE

Date:___/___/___

1. ***Realize***
   Describe your situation:

   _____
   _____
   _____
   _____
   _____
   _____
   _____

2. ***Reject***
   Which of the four fears does this trigger for you?

   •**The Fear of Failure:** *I must meet certain standards in order to feel good about myself.*

   •**The Need to be Punished:** *Those who fail (including myself) are unworthy of love and deserve to be punished.*

   •**The Fear of Rejection:** *I must be approved by certain others to feel good about myself.*

   •**The Feeling of Shame:** *I am what I am. I cannot change. I am hopeless.*

3. ***Replace***
   a) What characteristic of Christ helps overcome this fear? Write out the Scriptures on a separate sheet.

   _____
   _____

_____
_____
_____
_____
_____

b) How can you apply this perfect characteristic to this particular problem?

_____
_____
_____
_____
_____
_____

c) List one or more times when the Lord has understood you completely when you faced this problem:

_____
_____
_____
_____
_____
_____

d) List occasions when you were deceived, believing that God didn't understand you when you faced this problem:

_____
_____
_____
_____
_____
_____

e) Confess (agree) that your perception of Him was wrong when you were deceived, and then praise Him for understanding you and for giving you love, forgiveness, and power.

_____

_____

_____

_____

_____

_____

DAY THIRTEEN

Date:__/__/__

1. *Realize*
   Describe your situation:

   _____
   _____
   _____
   _____
   _____
   _____
   _____

2. *Reject*
   Which of the four fears does this trigger for you?

   •**The Fear of Failure:** *I must meet certain standards in order to feel good about myself.*

   •**The Need to be Punished:** *Those who fail (including myself) are unworthy of love and deserve to be punished.*

   •**The Fear of Rejection:** *I must be approved by certain others to feel good about myself.*

   •**The Feeling of Shame:** *I am what I am. I cannot change. I am hopeless.*

3. *Replace*
   a) What characteristic of Christ helps overcome this fear? Write out the Scriptures on a separate sheet.

   _____
   _____

_____
_____
_____
_____
_____

b) How can you apply this perfect characteristic to this particular problem?

_____
_____
_____
_____
_____
_____

c) List one or more times when the Lord has understood you completely when you faced this problem:

_____
_____
_____
_____
_____
_____

d) List occasions when you were deceived, believing that God didn't understand you when you faced this problem:

_____
_____
_____
_____
_____
_____

e) Confess (agree) that your perception of Him was wrong when you were deceived, and then praise Him for understanding you and for giving you love, forgiveness, and power.

_____

_____

_____

_____

_____

_____

_____

DAY FOURTEEN

Date:__/__/__

1. *Realize*
Describe your situation:

_____
_____
_____
_____
_____
_____
_____

2. *Reject*
Which of the four fears does this trigger for you?

• **The Fear of Failure:** *I must meet certain standards in order to feel good about myself.*

• **The Need to be Punished:** *Those who fail (including myself) are unworthy of love and deserve to be punished.*

• **The Fear of Rejection:** *I must be approved by certain others to feel good about myself.*

• **The Feeling of Shame:** *I am what I am. I cannot change. I am hopeless.*

3. *Replace*
a) What characteristic of Christ helps overcome this fear? Write out the Scriptures on a separate sheet.

_____
_____

_____
_____
_____
_____
_____

b) How can you apply this perfect characteristic to this particular problem?

_____
_____
_____
_____
_____

c) List one or more times when the Lord has understood you completely when you faced this problem:

_____
_____
_____
_____
_____
_____

d) List occasions when you were deceived, believing that God didn't understand you when you faced this problem:

_____
_____
_____
_____
_____

e) Confess (agree) that your perception of Him was wrong when you were deceived, and then praise Him for understanding you and for giving you love, forgiveness, and power.

_____

_____

_____

_____

_____

_____

_____

DAY FIFTEEN

Date:__/__/__

1. *Realize*
   Describe your situation:

   _____

   _____

   _____

   _____

   _____

   _____

   _____

2. *Reject*
   Which of the four fears does this trigger for you?

   •**The Fear of Failure:** *I must meet certain standards in order to feel good about myself.*

   •**The Need to be Punished:** *Those who fail (including myself) are unworthy of love and deserve to be punished.*

   •**The Fear of Rejection:** *I must be approved by certain others to feel good about myself.*

   •**The Feeling of Shame:** *I am what I am. I cannot change. I am hopeless.*

3. *Replace*
   a) What characteristic of Christ helps overcome this fear? Write out the Scriptures on a separate sheet.

   _____

   _____

_____

_____

_____

_____

_____

b) How can you apply this perfect characteristic to this particular problem?

_____

_____

_____

_____

_____

_____

c) List one or more times when the Lord has understood you completely when you faced this problem:

_____

_____

_____

_____

_____

_____

d) List occasions when you were deceived, believing that God didn't understand you when you faced this problem:

_____

_____

_____

_____

_____

_____

e) Confess (agree) that your perception of Him was wrong when you were deceived, and then praise Him for understanding you and for giving you love, forgiveness, and power.

_____

_____

_____

_____

_____

_____

_____

DAY SIXTEEN

Date:__/__/__

1. *Realize*
Describe your situation:

_____

_____

_____

_____

_____

_____

_____

2. *Reject*
Which of the four fears does this trigger for you?

• **The Fear of Failure:** *I must meet certain standards in order to feel good about myself.*

• **The Need to be Punished:** *Those who fail (including myself) are unworthy of love and deserve to be punished.*

• **The Fear of Rejection:** *I must be approved by certain others to feel good about myself.*

• **The Feeling of Shame:** *I am what I am. I cannot change. I am hopeless.*

3. *Replace*
a) What characteristic of Christ helps overcome this fear? Write out the Scriptures on a separate sheet.

_____

_____

_____
_____
_____
_____
_____

b) How can you apply this perfect characteristic to this particular problem?

_____
_____
_____
_____
_____
_____

c) List one or more times when the Lord has understood you completely when you faced this problem:

_____
_____
_____
_____
_____

d) List occasions when you were deceived, believing that God didn't understand you when you faced this problem:

_____
_____
_____
_____
_____

e) Confess (agree) that your perception of Him was wrong when you were deceived, and then praise Him for understanding you and for giving you love, forgiveness, and power.

_____

_____

_____

_____

_____

_____

_____

DAY SEVENTEEN

Date:__/__/__

1.   *Realize*
Describe your situation:

_____

_____

_____

_____

_____

_____

_____

2.   *Reject*
Which of the four fears does this trigger for you?

•**The Fear of Failure:** *I must meet certain standards in order to feel good about myself.*

•**The Need to be Punished:** *Those who fail (including myself) are unworthy of love and deserve to be punished.*

•**The Fear of Rejection:** *I must be approved by certain others to feel good about myself.*

•**The Feeling of Shame:** *I am what I am. I cannot change. I am hopeless.*

3.   *Replace*
a) What characteristic of Christ helps overcome this fear? Write out the Scriptures on a separate sheet.

_____

_____

_____

_____

_____

_____

_____

b) How can you apply this perfect characteristic to this particular problem?

_____

_____

_____

_____

_____

_____

c) List one or more times when the Lord has understood you completely when you faced this problem:

_____

_____

_____

_____

_____

_____

d) List occasions when you were deceived, believing that God didn't understand you when you faced this problem:

_____

_____

_____

_____

_____

_____

e) Confess (agree) that your perception of Him was wrong when you were deceived, and then praise Him for understanding you and for giving you love, forgiveness, and power.

_____

_____

_____

_____

_____

_____

_____

DAY EIGHTEEN

Date:___/___/___

1. *Realize*
   Describe your situation:

   _____
   _____
   _____
   _____
   _____
   _____
   _____

2. *Reject*
   Which of the four fears does this trigger for you?

   • **The Fear of Failure:** *I must meet certain standards in order to feel good about myself.*

   • **The Need to be Punished:** *Those who fail (including myself) are unworthy of love and deserve to be punished.*

   • **The Fear of Rejection:** *I must be approved by certain others to feel good about myself.*

   • **The Feeling of Shame:** *I am what I am. I cannot change. I am hopeless.*

3. *Replace*
   a) What characteristic of Christ helps overcome this fear? Write out the Scriptures on a separate sheet.

   _____
   _____

_____
_____
_____
_____
_____

b) How can you apply this perfect characteristic to this particular problem?

_____
_____
_____
_____
_____
_____

c) List one or more times when the Lord has understood you completely when you faced this problem:

_____
_____
_____
_____
_____
_____

d) List occasions when you were deceived, believing that God didn't understand you when you faced this problem:

_____
_____
_____
_____
_____

e) Confess (agree) that your perception of Him was wrong when you were deceived, and then praise Him for understanding you and for giving you love, forgiveness, and power.

_____

_____

_____

_____

_____

_____

_____

DAY NINETEEN

Date:__/__/__

1. *Realize*
Describe your situation:

_____

_____

_____

_____

_____

_____

_____

2. *Reject*
Which of the four fears does this trigger for you?

• **The Fear of Failure:** *I must meet certain standards in order to feel good about myself.*

• **The Need to be Punished:** *Those who fail (including myself) are unworthy of love and deserve to be punished.*

• **The Fear of Rejection:** *I must be approved by certain others to feel good about myself.*

• **The Feeling of Shame:** *I am what I am. I cannot change. I am hopeless.*

3. *Replace*
a) What characteristic of Christ helps overcome this fear? Write out the Scriptures on a separate sheet.

_____

_____

_____

_____

_____

_____

_____

b) How can you apply this perfect characteristic to this particular problem?

_____

_____

_____

_____

_____

_____

c) List one or more times when the Lord has understood you completely when you faced this problem:

_____

_____

_____

_____

_____

_____

d) List occasions when you were deceived, believing that God didn't understand you when you faced this problem:

_____

_____

_____

_____

_____

_____

e) Confess (agree) that your perception of Him was wrong when you were deceived, and then praise Him for understanding you and for giving you love, forgiveness, and power.

_____

_____

_____

_____

_____

_____

_____

DAY TWENTY

Date:__/__/__

1. *Realize*

Describe your situation:

_____

_____

_____

_____

_____

_____

_____

2. *Reject*

Which of the four fears does this trigger for you?

• **The Fear of Failure:** *I must meet certain standards in order to feel good about myself.*

• **The Need to be Punished:** *Those who fail (including myself) are unworthy of love and deserve to be punished.*

• **The Fear of Rejection:** *I must be approved by certain others to feel good about myself.*

• **The Feeling of Shame:** *I am what I am. I cannot change. I am hopeless.*

3. *Replace*

a) What characteristic of Christ helps overcome this fear? Write out the Scriptures on a separate sheet.

_____

_____

_____
_____
_____
_____
_____

b) How can you apply this perfect characteristic to this particular problem?

_____
_____
_____
_____
_____

c) List one or more times when the Lord has understood you completely when you faced this problem:

_____
_____
_____
_____
_____

d) List occasions when you were deceived, believing that God didn't understand you when you faced this problem:

_____
_____
_____
_____
_____

e) Confess (agree) that your perception of Him was wrong when you were deceived, and then praise Him for understanding you and for giving you love, forgiveness, and power.

_____

_____

_____

_____

_____

_____

_____

Rapha

Christ-centered Hospital and Counseling Care

*D*ear Friend,

In my heart, I feel that many people who read this book will be suffering from serious emotional or substance abuse problems or they will know someone who is. If so, I want them to know that there's hope.

You might be suffering yourself. And if you are, I want to assure you that there's hope for you, too, regardless of how serious your problems might be.

Our organization, RAPHA, provides Christ-centered treatment in hospitals and other settings where caring, committed professionals are seeing people of all ages healed of some of the most severe problems imaginable. The success stories we hear from children, youth and adults are indeed thrilling.

I want to encourage you to read the following pages very carefully. You will find information that will answer questions you might have about RAPHA and tell you more about the wide range of services we offer.

If you, personally, need help, or if you want to help someone, give us a call at 1-800-227-2657. Your inquiry will be strictly confidential.

Remember, we're here to serve you and to offer hope.

In Christ,

Robert S. McGee
President

"It has been good to know that we now have a place to refer persons we counsel who are in need of hospital care for emotional, spiritual and substance abuse problems."

Dr. Jerry Falwell
Pastor, Thomas Road Baptist Church
Founder, Old-Time Gospel Hour
Chancellor, Liberty University
Lynchburg, Virginia

"For years our churches have needed an anointed referral center to minister to those whose needs lie beyond the church counseling center. RAPHA is the answer."

Dr. Jimmy Draper
Pastor, First Baptist Church
Euless, Texas
Past President of the Southern Baptist Convention

*"S*urely the ministry of RAPHA has been blessed by God! Christians everywhere should rejoice that there is such a program available in this country!"

T. W. Wilson
Associate to Billy Graham
Billy Graham Evangelistic Association

"I appreciate the commitment that RAPHA has for the American teenager. RAPHA's treatment program comes from a biblical perspective and has brought about true healing for emotional needs."

Dawson McAllister
President, Shepherd Productions
Irving, Texas

"RAPHA is an excellent balance of clinical and spiritual. They are treating needs in a unique and dynamic way."

Ben Kinchlow
Author/Speaker

"There has been a great need for treatment with a sound spiritual perspective. RAPHA offers that kind of program."

Pat Boone
*Actor, Singer, Author and
Chairman of the National Easter Seal Society*

"RAPHA is committed to healing broken lives. I give it my heartiest endorsement and pray that God will use this ministry significantly."

Dr. Lewis A. Drummond
President, Southeastern Baptist Theological Seminary
Wake Forest, North Carolina

"I have longed for a Christ-centered ministry that addresses problems without sacrificing biblical principles. I believe RAPHA is such a program."

Dr. Adrian Rogers
Pastor, Bellevue Baptist Church
Memphis, Tennessee
Past President of the Southern Baptist Convention

True stories of God's miracles through RAPHA

Depression

"After 21 years of depression and having been on several types of treatment units, I am at last finally free from depression. The RAPHA unit is a place where you can meet God face to face."

"I was about as far down as I could go. I thank RAPHA for its support, concern and patience. Thanks for lifting me up to higher ground!"

"I truly thank our wonderful Lord for RAPHA. I've been feeling just great! I have suddenly noticed the beautiful world around me and look up toward heaven to thank the Lord for the beautiful trees and grass and the singing birds. For so long--three years--while I was going through depression I never noticed the beauty around me! Isn't God great?"

RAPHA ministers to adults and adolescents.

Chemical Dependency

RAPHA has taught me so much. I'm not preaching to my friends that use drugs; I'm just being an example of how you can deal with your problems instead of using drugs as an escape."

"The RAPHA program is great! I'm doing so well and have had no trouble staying away from drugs."

"We want to express our appreciation to you for all the help you have given our family resulting in the admission of our son to your facility and for helping him to overcome his alcohol addiction."

Eating Disorders

"For over 17 years I had bulimia and was ready to take my life. If it were not for RAPHA, I would still have this terrible eating disorder. I'm a changed person; I'm a confident person with more self-esteem than I've ever had with a good positive attitude about life. I now realize that God loves me deeply, completely forgives me, that I'm fully pleasing to Him, totally acceptable to Him, and am complete in Christ. I like me. I now understand that I don't need to earn love, that I'm worthy to be loved, just as I am for who I am."

RAPHA provides general psychiatric and substance abuse treatment.

Other Disorders

- Suicidal and/or homicidal ideations or attempts
- Noticeable negative changes in behavior
- Poor impulse control (stealing, aggression, etc.)
- Violent outbursts toward others
- Progressive or extreme withdrawal
- Disordered, unmanageable behaviors
- Imminent failure of social, familial, or occupational functioning
- Mania

- Psychosis
- Paranoia, phobias
- Periods of confusion
- Severe loss of memory
- Delusional systems (hallucinations)
- Uncontrollably obsessive thoughts
- Anxiety attacks
- Multiple personality manifestations
- Impairment of thoughts, judgment, logic or reality testing
- Inability to carry out activities of daily living

Call RAPHA
Toll Free, 24 hours a day
1-800-227-2657

Confidentiality is guaranteed.

What happens when you call RAPHA?

1. Evaluation will be made to determine if the person would benefit from one of RAPHA's programs.

2. The various treatment programs will be explained.

3. Financial aid and insurance availability will be explained.

4. If one of our programs is selected, admissions issues will be worked out prior to arrival at the treatment location. This includes travel aid, if needed.

To Order Additional Products

In addition to *The Parent Factor*, **Rapha Publishing** also offers the books, *The Search for Significance* and *How to Discipline with Love* by Robert S. McGee, founder and president of Rapha, and *Codependency* by Pat Springle.

Pricing

Title	Unit Price	Qty.	Total
The Parent Factor	$9.95	_____	$ _____
Codependency	7.95	_____	$ _____
Codependency Small Group Leader's Guide	3.00	_____	$ _____
The Search for Significance (book only)	6.00	_____	$ _____
The Search for Significance Book and Workbook	12.00	_____	$ _____
The Search for Significance Small Group Leader's Guide	3.00	_____	$ _____
How to Discipline with Love	4.00	_____	$ _____

Sub-Total $ _____
*Sales Tax $ _____
**Shipping & Handling $ _____
TOTAL $ _____

*6.5% Sales Tax - CA Residents only
**Shipg. & Hand. Min. Charge--$1.75 first book; $1.00 each additional book

Name:_____

Address:_____

City, State:_____

Zip:_____Phone: (   )_____

Send this order form and a check or money order for the total to:

R A P H A   P U B L I S H I N G
P.O. Box 580355
HOUSTON, TEXAS 77258